**JIM WINTER**

# Depression:
# a rescue plan

A practical Christian response to depression

DayOne

© Day One Publications 2000
First printed 2000
Reprinted 2004

Scripture quotations are from The New King James Version.
© 1982 Thomas Nelson Inc.

British Library Cataloguing in Publication Data available
ISBN 1 903087 03 1

Published by Day One Publications
Ryelands Road  Leominster  HR6 8NZ
☎ 01568 613 740
FAX: 01568 611 473
email  sales@dayone.co.uk
www.dayone.co.uk

Designed by Steve Devane and printed by CPD Wales

## Acknowledgements

To Clive and Amanda Anderson for their invaluable help from the conception to the delivery of this book.

To Derek Prime for providing a quotation from his sermon on John 21.

To Lynn Orr for allowing me to use her personal testimony.

To the deacons and members of Ealing Road Baptist Church for their patience and encouragement.

**Jim Winter, April 2000**

# Contents

# Introduction

It has been described as, 'the common cold of psychiatric medicine', and, 'the measles and mumps of the soul'. Winston Churchill referred to it as his 'black dog', and Samuel Johnson called it, 'this vile melancholy'. When in its grip, Abraham Lincoln described himself as, 'the most miserable man living'.

Depression is no respecter of persons. According to the World Health Organisation, 100 million people are depressed at any one time. During the decade before the close of the millennium, the number of people in the United Kingdom consulting their doctors complaining of depression more than doubled. This alarming increase may be due to the stresses of modern life, but it is more likely that many were not depressed at all, they were simply unhappy!

Herein lies the problem we face when dealing with the subject. The word 'depression' is used to describe a range of emotions and conditions from momentary unhappiness to suicidal despair. To complicate matters, its cause and effect encompass every area of our being. It is a medical issue, a psychological issue and a spiritual issue. In most cases it is a permutation of all three!

The problem intensifies when the depressed person is a Christian. We could argue that many people are depressed because their present has lost its meaning and purpose, and their future holds no hope. The Christian, however, has a living relationship with God in Jesus Christ, and the glorious anticipation of heaven! Yet, Christians *do* become depressed. For many, this is a devastating experience. Their depressed condition seems to stand in direct conflict with their faith and witness. It is not long before they are asking themselves, 'How can I be a Christian, if I am depressed?' As we shall see in the following pages, however, the lives of some of God's greatest servants clearly show that even the most godly person can become depressed.

Before I entered the Christian ministry, I earned my living repairing jewellery. I often had to untangle tightly knotted chains before I was able to mend them. Sometimes there would be two or three knotted together. To untangle a chain I would lay it on a flat surface and gently stroke the knotted area with two pins or needles. The act of stroking loosened the knots and enabled me to complete the job with my fingers. Understanding depression is like trying to untangle a chain of factors and permutations that have become tightly knotted together.

This book is written with the intention of doing that. The earlier chapters examine the causes and effects of depression. Later on we will look at ways in which we can prevent its onset and diminish its effect, and what to do if we become depressed and need help.

I am deeply aware of how little we still know about the causes of depression, but, after twenty years as an evangelical pastor, ministering to the depressed, I am equally aware of the wonderful grace of God and the perfect wisdom of the Bible. Depression may be a devastating experience, but it can also be a positive, even transforming, one. For many it will be a great trial, but we can take comfort in God's promise, 'That the genuineness of your faith, *being* much more precious than gold that perishes, though it is tested by fire, may be found to praise, honour, and glory at the revelation of Jesus Christ'(1 Peter 1:7).

Throughout this book, the masculine third person singular 'he' is interchangeable with the feminine 'she', unless the context requires a specific gender.

# Describing depression

I have given up trying to play golf. It seemed such a simple game whenever I took the club in my hand and made a few practice swings. It came down in a perfect arc, decapitating the daisy or whatever else I had chosen as my target. My problem occurred when I addressed the ball. I tried to remember the advice I had been given and the books I had read on golfing technique. I made sure that I had adopted the right stance and that my left shoulder was pointing towards the target. My mind computed all the factors that made a good golf shot and passed them on to my body. From time to time the ball landed in the intended place; but usually it scurried along the ground for about fifty yards and ended up in the rough! Where did I go wrong? My playing partners thought they knew, and were not slow in coming forward with advice. Each had his pet theory. Eventually, I made a decision. I would get some professional tuition and practise more, or give up. As I did not have the money or time for the former, I chose the latter.

Depression can be like that. We know what it takes to have a healthy, balanced life. We have tried to do the right things, but somehow we have ended up in the rough, and don't know why. Others think they do—and we are bombarded with well meaning but conflicting advice. Everything seems so simple to those who are not in our situation. They cannot understand why we cannot see it ourselves. It is possible that one of them is right—but which one? We decide that we will have to get help or give up. Our lives are infinitely more important than golf, so before we are tempted to give up, let's take time to examine the tangled chain that lays before us, and see if we can begin unravelling it.

The book of Job is a good place to start when we are trying to describe depression. It opens with the introduction of its main character: 'There was a man in the land of Uz, whose name was Job; and that man was blameless and upright, and one who feared God and shunned evil' (Job 1:1). Here was a man who seemed to have got everything right, yet his whole world collapsed around him. One by one the things that had enriched his life were taken from him—his wealth, his loved ones, and finally, his health. Job was bombarded with advice from those who thought they knew the cause and cure of his condition. Though he clung to his faith in God, he even cursed the day on which he was born (Job 3:1). Job described his feelings in the following way, 'For sighing comes before I eat'. And my groanings pour out like water. For the thing I greatly feared has come upon me. And what I dreaded has happened to me. I am not at ease, nor am I quiet; I have no rest, for trouble comes'. (Job 3:24-26).

Job is experiencing many of the feelings that we would associate with being depressed. These feelings are being expressed in every part of his being.

He is *physically* affected, 'For sighing comes before I eat.' And my groanings pour out like water.' This is exactly what happens to us when we are depressed. Involuntary sighs and groans become frequent as we are faced with essential day to day activities. Appetites are blunted, and even when we do eat we choose things that have little nutritional value. When we wash and put on clean clothes, we do so for the benefit of others; for we have lost interest in our physical appearance. Healthy patterns have become meaningless chores.

Job is also *mentally* affected. Fear and dread have taken his thoughts captive. Notice his feeling of total helplessness, 'For the thing I greatly feared has come upon me; And what I dreaded has happened to me'. This is something that has happened to him. It has come upon him and taken over his mind. When we are worried or anxious we try to push such thoughts to the back of our minds and concentrate on work or some other pressing need. We try to relax our minds by reading or concentrating on a film or a piece of music. We try to sleep, and if sleep comes, it is only fitful. However, in the normal run of things, this does not last long. The causes for worry or anxiety pass and we are back to our normal patterns of concentration and relaxation—but, when we are depressed it is a different matter. This feeling of fear and dread takes hold of us and we wonder whether it will ever let us go.

There is also a *spiritual* dimension to Job's condition. He is a man who 'feared God and shunned evil'. Surely there must be a place deep within his spirit where he can find rest from the turmoil of his physical and mental condition? Yet he says, 'I am not at ease, nor am I quiet; I have no rest, for trouble comes'. Faith and feeling are in conflict with each other. Job clearly knows that his destiny is in the hand of God. His faith will not be shaken, yet he finds it hard to absorb this truth into his present condition. Here is one of the great problems that we face when dealing with depression. We can accept that our bodies and minds will undergo stress and conflict as we go through life—but surely our faith will always rise above such things? Ultimately it will; but when we are depressed the great fact of salvation is often buried beneath intense feelings of guilt, doubt and fear.

We could argue that Job's position is unique and that the circumstances in which he finds himself are far removed from ours! This is true, but there is, in the story of Job, a valid illustration of the way in which depression affects a person. Anyone suffering depression, for whatever reason, can relate to Job's all consuming debilitating condition. Such a condition may vary in intensity and duration, but the physical, mental and spiritual factors are always present.

How do people experiencing depression describe their feelings? We will take two examples. Firstly, a young mother of four children, 'Depression is a world of paradoxes: feeling empty, but being full with every emotion; wanting to die, but wanting to live to the full; always feeling tired, yet never sleeping; wanting to be loved and accepted, yet being unable to love fully and accept properly. The worst thing about depression, for me, is the total loss of identity. You no longer know who you are. The person you are is lost in a soup of confusion. It's like looking in a mirror and seeing no reflection—you feel that you no longer exist. Maybe that is why it is easy for someone who is depressed to take their own life.'

And secondly, a famous writer and comedian undergoing psychiatric treatment for clinical depression: 'It's rather as though you are sitting with an eiderdown over you and you hear the doorbell ring and you think, 'I'll have to go and answer that' And you struggle, but to little avail. You can, perhaps, just about go but it is a terrible effort because this wretched eiderdown just drags you back and down and smothers you.[1]

We have looked at the way in which people have described their feelings of depression. We will now proceed to describe depression itself.

The New English Dictionary describes depression as, 'lowering of the spirits, dejection, lacking in energy and activity'. It then goes on to list some of the ways in which the word is used in specific areas. I include these because they each give a graphic metaphor of the way in which we can describe the feeling of depression: *Astronomy*, 'the angular distance of a heavenly body below the horizon'; *meteorology*, 'a low state of the barometer indicative of bad weather'; *military*, 'the lowering of the muzzle of a gun'; *music*, 'lowering of pitch, flattening'. Do not all these uses of the word 'depression' strike a chord in the heart and mind of the depressed person? When it appears that God has slipped below the horizon and is no longer there—when you are under a cloud and the forecast seems even bleaker—when you feel that you can no longer fight this thing and lower the muzzle of your gun—when everything seems flat and out of tune.

## A psychological description of depression

Psychologists are more specific when they describe depression. Depression is, 'A mood state characterized by a sense of inadequacy, a feeling of despondency, a decrease in activity and reactivity, pessimism, sadness and related symptoms.' A psychiatric definition treats the above as, 'An affective disorder in which the symptoms... are extreme or intense.'[2]

One level treats depression as a 'mood state'; the other as an 'affective disorder'. In other words, one is describing depression in terms of, 'This is how I *feel*', and the other in terms of, 'This is how I *am*'. As John White has put it, '*Mood* represents the emotional weather whereas *affect* represents the climate.'[3] The difference between the two is determined by the degree of intensity and the effect of the condition on the personality. Depression operates on a wide scale. Imagine a vertical scale. At the top we have a form of depression which most people experience from time to time—it does not last long and we are soon back on song. At the bottom is the heavy eiderdown that covers you—the black cloud of despair that seems never ending. The difference between the two conditions is found, not so much in the cause or symptoms, but in the intensity and effect of the depression itself. In one case a person may describe their condition by saying, 'This is how I feel', but someone with the same symptoms, because they are so intense and widespread, has to say, 'This is how I am'.

Herein lies one of the great dangers and difficulties when dealing with depression. We must ask, 'Am I dealing with a mood or a condition?' The answer will not always be the same. This leads us on into another problem area. Is there a point along the scale where a mood becomes a condition? This is one of the great difficulties facing those who are seeking to help the depressed. Great wisdom is needed in determining the intensity and extent of the condition. The problem for the caring professionals is summed up by Mark Radcliffe, the Mental Health Editor of the Nursing Times: 'Depression is a terrible thing—like treacle on the soul.' It is crippling, life threatening and debilitating. Unhappiness isn't any of these things. It is just like sadness, but longer. Where is the line between unhappiness and depression? What if we get the line wrong? Are we not, perhaps, pathologising and medicalising normal human emotions simply because we don't like them much? 4

## A Biblical description of depression

Depression is a relatively new word for a condition that has afflicted man throughout his history. Older medical and psychological text-books generally refer to it as 'melancholia'. After consulting the distinguished seventeenth century doctor, Sir Thomas Mayerne, Oliver Cromwell was diagnosed as 'valde melancholicus'—extremely melancholy.

The Bible uses neither word, but has much to say about the condition. Words like: despair (Ecclesiastes 2:20); dismay (Joshua 1:9); discouraged (Colossians 3:21); distress (1 Samuel 28:15); downcast (Job 22:29); sorrow (Exodus 3:7); and sighing (Ezekiel 21:6,7) describe the extent to which the mind of man is troubled by his circumstances.

Biblical biography furnishes us with other pictures. Contemplating the capture and destruction of Jerusalem, Jeremiah says, 'My soul. . . sinks within me. . . Therefore I have no hope.'(Lamentations 3:20-21). Nehemiah's depressed expression prompted King Artaxerxes to say, 'Why is your face sad, since you are not sick?' This is nothing but sorrow of heart.'(Nehemiah 2:2). Unable to bear children, Hannah became so distraught she could not eat. 'She *was* in bitterness of soul, and prayed to the Lord and wept in anguish.'(1 Samuel 1:10). Jesus addressed the travellers on the road to Emmaus with the words, 'What kind of conversation *is* this that you have with one another as you walk and are sad?'(Luke 24:17). Moses (Numbers 11:15) and Elijah (1 Kings 19:4) both prayed that they might die. Even the Lord Jesus Christ, 'A Man of sorrows and acquainted with grief', felt 'sorrowful and deeply distressed' in Gethsemene (Matthew 26:37).

The Psalms abound with expressions that we can easily relate to the experience of depression: 'I am troubled, I am bowed down greatly; I go mourning all the day long. . . I groan because of the turmoil of my heart. . . my sorrow is continually before me.'(Psalm 38:6, 8, 17); '*having* sorrow in my heart daily'(Psalm 13:2); my groaning all the day long. . . My vitality was turned into the drought of summer.'(Psalm 32:3-4); 'When they are diminished and brought low Through oppression, affliction and sorrow.'(Psalm 107:39).

We can see from these Scriptures—and there are a good deal more—that many of the things that we would relate to *depression* are part of life for both saint and sinner. Referring to the title of Psalm 102, 'A Prayer of the afflicted, when he is overwhelmed and pours out his complaint before the Lord', William Bridge says, 'This is so ordinary a case, that the Holy Ghost has provided a standing psalm, or prayer, on purpose for such as are in this condition.'[5]

In the Psalm 42 David deals with a condition that bears many of the characteristics of depression. C. H. Spurgeon likens it to 'the voice of a spiritual believer, under depressions, longing for the renewal of the divine presence, struggling with doubts and fears, but yet holding his ground by faith in the living God.'[6]

David describes his condition in the following way: 'Why are you cast down, O my soul? And why are you disquieted within me?' This is repeated three times, in verses 5 and 11 of Psalm 42, and in verse 5 of Psalm 43. It is helpful to examine the words he uses to describe his condition—'cast down' and 'disquieted'.

In the original Hebrew the word translated, 'cast down' means to sink or depress, bend, bow down, to humble. 'Disquieted' means to make a loud noise or tumult, to rage, to war, moan, clamour—to be troubled. These words describe two very different aspects of David's condition. One is passive the other is active. In one sense he is cast down—bent low, oppressed and wrapped in an eiderdown that weighs heavily upon him. He cannot seem to move or breathe; he feels trapped. Deep inside, instead of being passive, he is deeply stirred and troubled. He is disquieted. This is the reversal of his normal condition. By nature David is a doer. A man who throws himself, heart and soul, into the task that lies before him. He is also a man who, as a rule, is at one with God; a man who has a deep sense of peace within his heart. This is so often the case with those who are depressed. Human emotions are turned upside down. Where we were once active we become passive. We lose interest in doing things—working, playing, exercising—we just want to sit and gaze into space. We want to stay in bed and bury our heads under the covers instead of facing the challenge of a new day. If we do get up we have little desire to wash and get dressed. Everything seems like a heavy weight upon us—we are 'cast down'- but inside, we are far from passive. The peace and sense of well-being that sustained us through our most active periods is gone. It is replaced by a feeling of agitation and fear, something akin to war, with nowhere to run and hide. Everything is inside out, back to front, and upside down—and it disturbs us deeply!

# Characteristics of depression

W e concluded the previous chapter with a description of depression from Psalms 42 and 43. In the same Psalms, David also shows some of its characteristics and symptoms. He sees a metaphor for his condition in the deer panting for the water brooks. The deer's body is still, yet its heart is pounding in its breast. The whole body of the deer is on the alert. It is tired, but it cannot relax because it is thirsty. The physical act of panting only serves to tire the animal and increase its thirst. It becomes a vicious circle of an increasing need for water and a decreasing strength to find it. Only the waterbrooks will enable the deer to survive. David feels truly deserted. He is undergoing a desert experience that can only be relieved by a deep sense of the presence of his God. He is exhausted but agitated. Stress seems to have taken its toll on him. His nervous system is up for the fight, but his limbs feel like lead, and there seems to be no waterbrook in sight. Has he got the energy to look for one? Loss of energy is a common characteristic of depression. We all experience periods of extreme tiredness, but in normal circumstances we can quickly regain our energy through rest and relaxation. Maybe we are so tired we need a good holiday, but on our return we are refreshed and equipped to pick up where we left off. But when we are depressed nothing seems able to stave off the feeling of total exhaustion. Our bodies are in a constant state of alert, unable to rest.

David is nostalgic for times past. His mind goes back to better days, 'For I used to go with the multitude; I went with them to the house of God, With the voice of joy and praise, With a multitude that kept a pilgrim feast.' When we are feeling depressed our minds often go back to better days; when we were able to join in with others in joy and celebration. Physical illness, age, circumstances, or even just our depressed condition, disable us in doing the things we once loved to do. Remembering the good times only serves to increase the sense of isolation and self-pity. We empathize with David when he says, 'When I remember these things, I pour out my soul within me'.

He feels deeply the oppression of his enemies. Twice they taunt him with the cry, 'Where is your God?' We do not know who these enemies are, but it may be that some of them are to be found inside his own head. Self accusation often accompanies depression. We become angry at ourselves for being depressed... which makes us more depressed... which makes us angrier... We feel that we must have the answer to our condition but feel confused and frustrated because we do not understand what is happening to us.

Like Job, David's faith and feelings are in direct conflict. This, as we shall see later in the book, will become a great factor in his deliverance. During the dark hours of such an experience this is the most debilitating and frightening factor—the power of present feelings seemingly overwhelming a faith that we were certain was built upon a solid rock.

Most, if not all, of us experience this in some degree from time to time. It is part of the experience that we call life. However, we struggle through, and by God's grace the gloom lifts and we are back in the sunshine. We are not harmed by the experience and if we are wise we value the lessons we have learned, but for some—sometimes—the feeling of depression holds them in a vice like grip from which there seems to be no possible escape.

What are the characteristics or symptoms that make us realize that we need help? In other words, what takes us below the threshold of sadness or unhappiness into what can only be described as a state of depression?

I am not a psychiatrist; therefore I am not qualified nor competent to assess the qualities of medical diagnosis. It is helpful, however, to look at the criteria used in diagnosing depression as a medical condition. The following list is taken from the *Diagnostic and Statistical Manual of Mental Disorders (American Psychiatric Association 1994)*. To be diagnosed as depressed, a patient must have experienced these symptoms for at least two weeks:

▶ Depressed mood most of the day, nearly every day;
▶ Markedly diminished interest or pleasure in all or most activities, most of the day, nearly every day.

Four of these symptoms must be present during the same period:
▶ Significant weight-loss or gain or decrease or increase in appetite;
▶ Insomnia;
▶ Psychomotor agitation or retardation;
▶ Fatigue or loss of energy;

- Feelings of worthlessness or excessive/inappropriate guilt (with or without delusions);
- Diminished ability to think or concentrate or indecisiveness;
- Recurrent thoughts of death or recurrent suicidal ideas with or without specific plans or recent suicide attempt.

It is important for us to understand that very few of us will experience depression that falls into the above category. For those who do, help is readily available and the prognosis is good! In a helpful book, published by the British Medical Association, Dr. Greg Wilkinson puts our minds at rest: 'As a rough guide, severe depression affects 3% to 4% of us, but only 20% of those affected see their doctor, of whom only 50% are treated by a psychiatrist. Only one person in 50 with a depressive illness needs hospital treatment.'[1]

In his book, *Overcoming Depression: A practical self-help guide to prevention and treatment*, the psychiatrist, Dr Richard Gillett lists five interrelated characteristics which help us make some kind of assessment as to whether we have gone beyond the 'This is how I *feel*' stage, to 'This is how I *am*'. The characteristics are: Emptiness rather than sadness; loss of energy; sulking or self-pity; giving up; and negative colouration.

Sadness is a normal part of life. It varies in intensity, generally in relationship to the event that causes it. At its lightest it is not an unpleasant feeling. Many people look forward to a trip to the cinema to watch a 'weepy'. At its heaviest it can be devastating. Bereavement is probably the saddest experience that we must all go through. The initial shock of knowing that we have lost someone dear to us, is followed by a sense of disbelief that it has really happened. Then the reality hits us and we are flooded with a deep sense of emotional turmoil. In the days, weeks and months to come we experience despair, pain, anger, guilt and love in varying intensities. There is a feeling of emptiness, but it is a feeling that is being constantly expressed in the natural grief process. Although bereavement exhibits many of the characteristics of depression, and in some cases can lead on to depression, it is not, in itself, depression. It is deep sadness. As Gillett points out 'Sadness is active, depression is passive'[2]. In depression, a person is locked into a state of emptiness where feelings are rarely, if ever, expressed.

As we have already mentioned, loss of energy is a characteristic of depression. This is not restricted to a physical feeling of tiredness and lethargy. We lose the energy to feel and express emotions. We no longer have the energy to appreciate the sights, sounds, tastes and experiences that have enriched our lives. We lose interest in the things that once captured our attention, our work, our recreational activities, our friends, our homes. We do not want to make plans for the future. Sometimes we find it hard to concentrate and remember even the most recent event or conversation.

We all feel sorry for ourselves from time to time, when we feel that we have been misunderstood, or not appreciated by others. This feeling soon passes when we are able to think things through and get a balanced perspective. Talking to someone about our feelings often helps us see things clearly. However, we can easily turn our self-pity inward and start to sulk. We will not communicate our feelings to others; even deny that there is anything troubling us. We treat ourselves like helpless victims of circumstance. When we were children we may have sulked in order to get our own way. Sometimes it worked; sometimes it did not—but, we can remember the power of that sulk. Even when we wanted to come out of it and get back to normal relationships with others, we found that the sulk itself had a power over us that prevented us from taking the initiative. It was generally the patient friend or parent who broke the spell. Husbands and wives who have to endure the sulks of a partner know that sometimes it is even a matter of weeks before the relationship returns to normal. The person who is feeling sorry for himself sees himself as the victim. Very often, the root of this condition is a feeling of worthlessness or even excessive or inappropriate guilt. Self-pity becomes depression when we can no longer free ourselves from its grip—when we find it impossible to laugh at ourselves.

Giving up follows on from the victim scenario. As Gillett says, 'The process of depression involves a gradual abdication of responsibility'.3 Taking responsibility is part of our life process. Some people thrive on it; others are less comfortable with it. God has created us as responsible beings. We are responsible to Him for our lives and what we do with them. Parents are responsible for their children and, ultimately, children are responsible for their parents. In the body of Christ, the church, believers are responsible for each other's welfare and share a responsibility for the promulgation of the gospel to all mankind. When we are depressed we feel that we can no longer bear responsibility for anything, even ourselves. The temptation is to give up, and in the cases of deep depression there seems to be no alternative.

How we colour life depends very much on how we feel. Imagine for a moment that you were able to draw in pencil a series of pictures of the circumstances in which you find yourself. In doing so you can be reasonably objective. What you are putting on the paper are facts and concrete situations. In other words, the outline of life as it is for you at any particular moment. You are then asked to colour your picture. How you feel about each situation will be the determining factor on which colours you use. Take one picture. The circumstances depicted may present a new opportunity that conjures up for you a feeling of excitement. You colour it bright yellow. However, the same circumstance may have the opposite effect. You may feel threatened by it, so you colour it black. Whatever colour you choose the basic outline stays the same. You may even reach a conclusion that there is no need to colour any of the pictures as life itself has no colour. When we are depressed we see things in greys, blacks and whites. There is no place for colour in any of our circumstance.

# Causes of depression (1)

Theories as to the causes of depression abound. A great deal of medical research has taken place to investigate the nature of biological changes in body chemistry that contribute to mood disorders. As a result of this, anti-depressant medication has been devised and used to some effect. Psychological theories are less defined and generally determined by particular theories of personality. Different schools of thought focus on different causes. A psychodynamic approach will focus on inward aggression and the loss of a 'love object'; while others will argue that depression is the result of a disturbance of cognition rather than emotion. The behaviourist sees it in terms of learned helplessness; while the existentialist as the loss of meaning of existence. This, of course, is an oversimplification of more complex theories, but it does illustrate the diversity of information and speculation that surrounds our subject. A biblical approach, while acknowledging the contribution of medicine and psychology, will inevitably cause us to look deeply at our relationship with God and his Word.

In the following two chapters we will look at some of the reasons why a person may become depressed. I will limit the field to reasons which generally apply to our human condition. In subsequent chapters we will deal with matters more specific to the Christian.

## Ruined by the fall

The origin of all pain and suffering of body and mind; of sin and death and estrangement from God; all the calamities of this life and the judgement to come, can be traced back to one event in the history of man—*the fall* (Genesis 3). As a result, every area of man's being, body and soul, has been corrupted by sin. Our bodies are subject to sickness and decay, and ultimately to death (Genesis 3:12; Romans 5:12; 6:23). Our thoughts and desires are permeated with rebellion against God (Genesis 6:5). The fall is central to our understanding of man's condition and the need for salvation in Jesus Christ. D. Martyn Lloyd-Jones describes it in the following way: 'The Bible tells us that God made the world, he made man. He placed male and female in a position that can be described as paradise. There they lived and had communion with God. You get an idyllic picture. Then you come on and get this other picture which is provided in this third chapter. It tells us of life as it was and then shows us this picture of Adam and Eve hiding in their misery and wretchedness, trying to avoid God and get away from that Voice that followed them. It announces the curse that came upon the earth—that the woman should conceive in sorrow and pain and that the man should toil and eat in the sweat of his face—and we are told how thorns and thistles, disease and death came in. First life as God made it; then life as it has become. There is the whole answer, the whole explanation of the position we are considering together.'[1]

Even the apostle Paul had to admit, 'For I know that in me (that is, in my flesh) nothing good dwells; for to will is present with me, but *how* to perform what is good I do not find.' (Romans 7:18). As a result of this, we are no longer, by nature, in communion with our Creator. In sin we are 'strangers from the covenants of promise, having no hope and without God in the world' (Ephesians 2:12). The first sin had an immediate effect on the consciences of Adam and Eve. They became aware of the pollution caused by their act of disobedience. Even before the Lord God had spoken they became aware of their guilt and shame (Genesis 3:7). We share that same consciousness with them. The great message of the gospel is that, in Jesus Christ, the last Adam, there is deliverance from the penalty of that original sin. By a living faith in Him, the severed relationship with God is restored, and instead of being under the sentence of spiritual death the believer rejoices in the gift of eternal life (Romans 6:23).

The Christian, however, still lives in a world of sin and a body which will one day experience the miracle of the resurrection, but for now is still subject to the effect of sin. In other words, citizens of the kingdom of God, while here on earth, are subject to the same physical phenomena and circumstances as those experienced by everybody else. We share a common humanity with others and the fall still has its effect upon us.

One of the common problems faced by the Christian as he addresses this matter of depression is the question, 'Should a Christian ever be depressed?' If depression is merely a matter of sinful behaviour and thinking, which can be quickly rectified by repentance and faith, the answer is, 'No, we should never be depressed.' But there is sufficient evidence to suggest that depression has causes within the effect of the fall that we are still experiencing along with all humanity. We accept the frailty of the human body, even the Son of God hungered and thirsted, and needed rest in his days in the flesh. Most Christians will accept that physical disease is part of life and that it is not necessarily a direct judgement of God upon personal sin, nor is its presence an indication of lack of faith for healing. Yet, even those who accept this truth draw the line when it comes to dealing with depression. As a result, the sufferer is urged to, 'Snap out of it', by a person who would not even dream of saying the same thing to a cancer victim or someone temporarily disabled by a broken leg. In this chapter we will address some of the evidence that depression is, indeed, a condition which can seriously be considered to result from the same source as many of the more obviously physical diseases to which we are subject.

## Physical factors

There are a number of physical factors thought to be important contributors to a state of depression. Firstly, a *chemical or hormonal imbalance*. This can be one which naturally occurs in the body such as, pre-menstrual tension, post natal depression, the menopause, or even seasonally affective disorder. Or this can be the side effects of medication, taken for an unrelated reason. A lack of oxygen to the brain can have bizarre effects on our state of mind. Even the ageing process brings with it an increasing likelihood of depressive tendencies.

Secondly, some *physical diseases* seem to induce depressive tendencies. The great Victorian preacher and pastor, Charles Haddon Spurgeon was a case in point. Spurgeon suffered from Bright's disease and severe bouts of deep depression. Many have linked the two. On one occasion he wrote, 'The furnace still glows around me. Since I last preached to you, I have been brought very low; my flesh has been tortured with pain, and my spirit has been prostrate with depression... I am as a potter's vessel when it is utterly broken, useless and laid aside. Nights of watching, and days of weeping have been mine, but I hope the cloud is passing'[2] The symptoms of depression may be masks for a physical disease. This is why the good GP will insist on a physical check up before going on to a diagnosis of depression itself.

Thirdly, *hereditory factors*. There is some evidence that certain kinds of depression are more likely to occur in some families than in others. This may be due to the presence of a depressive gene, although current research has yet to clearly identify this. One psychiatrist has described it as, 'looking for an ant on Mount Everest'.[3] On the other hand, the family environment may have a significant part to play in this.

Fourthly, *endogenous causes*; where depression can be considered as a disease in its own right. Endogenous simply means 'from within'. Here is depression at its most powerful and debilitating. It is at this point where medication and psychiatric treatment seem to provide the only answer.

## Temperament

There is little doubt that some people, by the very nature of their temperament, seem to be more prone to depression than others. The temperamental factor is an important one and must be addressed. However, we must proceed with caution. God has created us as unique individuals. As individuals we have temperamental tendencies. Some of us are adventurous, some are cautious; some need company, some are quite happy to be on their own; some are by nature optimistic, some are pessimistic. We see this clearly in biblical characters. The apostle Peter was temperamentally different from John or Paul. Elijah appeared to be a 'loner', whilst Elisha sought and enjoyed the company of others. David's temperament was of a very different nature to Joseph's. When considering the suitability of a candidate for service in the church, we are instructed to take the temperamental factor into account ( 1 Timothy 3:2; Titus 1:7,8). Recognising that we are all of a certain temperament, we must never adopt a position where we are governed by it. As we shall see in later chapters, there are actions we can take to control our temperaments and reduce their power over us. There is a tendency today to put people into categories and assume that they will behave accordingly.

From ancient times man has sought to classify human temperament into types. This predominately has its roots in astrology and the occult. Hippocrates and Galen were the first to introduce physical factors into the equation. We must remember, however, that, for them, medicine and astrology went hand in hand. Their theories were based on the four 'humours', or fluids, of the body; blood, phlegm; yellow bile, and black bile. On this basis, Galen divided the temperamental nature of man into, sanguine (stable and expression feeling), phlegmatic (stable and passive), choleric (unstable and excitable), and melancholic (unstable and paralysed with fear). This theory seemed to predominate in medicine for many centuries until dismissed as unscientific.

With the emergence of endocrinology in the early part of the twentieth century, the theories of correlation between temperament and body fluids has been revived. There have been attempts to classify temperament according to secretions of the ductless glands (adrenal, thyroid, parathyroid, gonads, and pituitary).

W H Sheldon, building on Ernst Kretschmer's theories on personality and body types classified body types as, endomorphs (round and soft with a predominate digestive system), mesmomorphs (wide-shouldered and hard with a predominate muscular system), and ectomorphs (delicately formed and linear with a predominate nervous system). Out of this he built three types of temperament corresponding with these physical features. The endomorph is a sociable person who is generally relaxed, and loves ease and comfort. A mesmomorph is vigorous and assertive, wanting to control situations and people. An ectomorph is restrained, inhibited, and hypersensitive; someone who keeps himself emotionally and socially at a distance from others.

The best known of all the psychological theories is the introvert/extrovert theory of Carl Gustav Jung. In *Modern Man in Search of a Soul*, he writes, 'Introversion and extroversion, as a typical attitude, means an essential bias which conditions the whole psychic process, establishes the habitual reactions, and thus determines not only the style of behaviour, but also the nature of the subjective experience. And not only so, but also denotes the kind of compensatory activity of the unconscious which we may expect to find.'[4] Jung's theories are the foundation for the Myers-Briggs Type Indicator that is widely used today, even in Christian circles. It is important to note that Jung was deeply interested in astrology and the occult.

Some theories on the causes of depression point to the hereditary causes, particularly those associated with temperament. The important thing is that God calls and uses people with all kinds of temperaments. Temperament is never a valid excuse for sin or unacceptable behaviour.

# Causes of depression (2)

In the previous chapter we looked at causes of depression that have their origin in our general state of being. We will now look at ways in which our external circumstances, and our response to them, affect our mood and condition.

## Stress

It is now thought that stress plays a significant factor in the onset of many diseases. Depression is no exception. Stress is an essential part of healthy living. In order to keep our bodies healthy we must place them under some kind of physical stress through exercise. In order to keep our minds healthy we must place them under stress by giving them information to store and problems to solve. Stress can be either a cause or an effect. As a cause it is used to modify the form of something. We use stress in order to shape things. The manufacture of an aeroplane must involve thousands of processes where stress is exerted upon components as they are made and assembled. Vast amounts of stress are needed to make it airborne and to keep it flying. The aeroplane is also subject to the stress as an effect. The very act of taking off, flying and landing, over a long period of time in varying conditions will take its toll. Stress will have a degenerative effect upon the structure of the aircraft and eventually it will be taken out of service and confined to the scrap heap.

We must address stress in the same two-fold way. Our lives are shaped by it. We have to be sure that it is coming from the right direction in order to shape our lives for the good and not the ill. For the Christian, the right source for positive stress is the Word of God. The precepts and commandments of God shape us into what He wants to make of us. We are like clay in the potter's hand. However, even the Christian feels the effect of other forces at work. For example, other people may try putting pressure on us to make us into what they want us to be. Sometimes the pressure comes from within as we rebel against the will of God. Can you imagine a piece of metal being hammered from all directions instead of one? What kind of shape would you expect it to be in? One of the best diagnostic questions we can ask ourselves when assessing the stress levels in our lives is, 'Who is in control?' Some people suffering from stress related illnesses have found that either their lives were being governed by others or by what seemed to them to be pure chance. Others were sure that they were in control but soon found that they had overestimated their capacity to cope. The Christian, however, should be able to have a balanced attitude to and experience of stress. Self-control is a fruit of the Holy Spirit (Galatians 5:23) and is something that we must never give up to another person. And, those things which are plainly outside of our control are safely in the Craftsman's hand, shaping and moulding us into what he would have us be, 'But we have this treasure in earthen vessels, that the excellence of the power may be of God and not of us. *We are* hard pressed on every side, yet not crushed; *we are* perplexed, but not in despair; persecuted, but not forsaken; struck down, but not destroyed—always carrying about in the body the dying of the Lord Jesus, that the life of Jesus also may be manifested in our body'(2 Corinthians 4:7-10).

Many of the factors we could have used under the previous heading can be great causes of stress. Overwork, lack of work, loss of self control, ageing, financial problems, guilt feelings. Destructive stress occurs when we find ourselves in a position where our commitments are greater than our ability or energy to fulfil them. It is as if our lives are run by everyone else but ourselves. Much of this can be our own fault. We have been unable to say no to requests from others. We have been over ambitious in our assessment of situations.

Whatever the reasons for our stressful condition, we may start to blame others for putting us under stress. Some of us may suffer from the 'martyr syndrome'. We want to be the ideal mother or father, pastor or church member. We determine, for ourselves, what others expect of us and throw ourselves into fulfilling those expectations. When we become tired or frustrated we become angry at those we serve for making unreasonable demands on us. We are angry at their apparent ingratitude! The Christian can even extend this into his relationship with God. We may, in theory, accept the fact that salvation is by grace through faith, but, in practice, we may set up an impossible spiritual regime that we feel will somehow compensate for the sin in our lives. When it does not work, we even end up blaming God for our condition. We can become resentful and begin to slip into the state of self-pity that we considered in chapter two.

## Circumstances of life

Life is not lived on an emotional plane. We experience highs and lows, and these are greatly determined by our circumstances. No one is in control of the people and events that surround him. Because of this, we have to go through periods when we are called upon to cope with emotional stress. As a rule we do not like change. Most of us develop routines that suit us. The nature of our employment may change; we may have to change our job; or we may even lose our job. We may have to move house or location. Not all of our relationships work out well. There will be times of tension between us and those we love dearly. As parents, we may have great difficulties with our teenage children. Eventually, those children leave home and the house feels empty. We also have to face personal failure and disappointment. We can never get it right all the time. For some of us this can be devastating, especially if we are perfectionists and have fallen short of the standards that we have set ourselves. Sometimes this failure is not our fault but the fault of others. This can make us angry and bitter at the unfairness of it all. As we mature, we learn to cope with such things. We accept that for a short time we will feel sad or unhappy with our lot, but that time will pass and we will get used to the new circumstances. At some time we have to cope with bereavement. Whatever pains we take to prepare for such an event it is still devastating. This is especially true when the death of the loved one is sudden and unexpected.

## Grief

Of all the circumstances of life grief is the one that takes us closest to depression. Grief itself is not depression. However painful, numbing, or disorientating the experience; it is a normal part of life in a world that has been contaminated with the law of sin and death. Bereavement is not a disease that needs to be cured. It is a road that needs to be travelled. However, the debilitating effect of any of these circumstances, particularly bereavement, can militate against our mental and physical well-being and contribute to a state of depression.

Grief, however, covers a much wider range than the death of a loved one. It is fundamentally a sense of loss. Something that contributed to our sense of security and well-being has been taken from us. Someone we relied upon, who we thought would always be there, has let us down or moved away. On the other hand, we may have been in a position where we felt useful and fulfilled and have been replaced by another. As a result we feel a loss of confidence and self-worth. It may be the loss of something that has brought comfort to us; a family pet, or a keepsake that reminded us of happier times. Whatever the loss, how trivial it may seem to others, it has threatened the safe routine of our lives.

Often, a combination of losses makes us feel that life is changing too rapidly for us to keep up. We feel a deep sense of vulnerability to the vicissitudes of life. If we are Christians, we will turn to our faith to sustain us and, because we often, falsely, equate faith with feelings, we will be left with a sense that we are even losing that! We must remind ourselves that the Bible teaches us that, 'In the world you will have tribulation'. We must not forget the promise that accompanies the stark fact of life, 'but be of good cheer, I have overcome the world' (John 16:33).

## Inappropriate reaction

A common cause for depression is an inappropriate reaction to events. This is known as 'reactive depression' and is generally used to describe the type of depression that does not seem to have an underlying physical cause. This is an area where preventative measures are most effective.

As we have already seen, we are constantly having to respond to the circumstances of life. Our response is generally in the form of a reaction. We experience the event; we process our perception of the event in the light of previously learned experience; our whole biochemistry becomes involved in this reaction. As a rule this involves little or no rational thought. The reaction is automatic. This is a God given quality that enables us to survive the dangers presented to us by our environment. Some refer to it as the 'fear, fight, flight mechanism'. You may be walking along the pavement lost in thought. As you are just about to step out into the road you are brought to your senses by the sound of an approaching car. In an instant you step back to the safety of the pavement. Your mind has perceived the situation; registered the fact that cars kill pedestrians; sent the appropriate message to your body and your body has performed the necessary safety manoeuvre. Such is the speed and intensity of the situation, even on the safety of the pavement your heart is beating fast and you feel faint.

However, many situations are not quite as simple as this. We have to respond to stimuli that are sometimes more complex and less life threatening. The process that saved us from being run over by the car does not always function as clearly and efficiently. People who suffer panic attacks often find that such attacks are triggered by seemingly innocuous situations. Something they see or hear—some particular change in their environment—may well cause them to immediately go into a state of panic. Let me give you a personal example. From time to time I suffer attacks of migraine. I well remember the first time this happened to me. I was driving in heavy traffic on a wet night. As I looked at the number plate of the car in front I noticed a flickering in the corner of my vision. As I looked again, I realized that I could not see all the number. My vision was becoming distorted. Although I could still see clearly, my brain did not seem able to register everything as a complete picture. I must confess that I was frightened at what was happening to me. I had never experienced anything like it before. By the time I arrived home I was in a state of panic. I was sweating and trembling. I remember lying on my bed trying to make my eyes work properly by focusing on objects in the room. I tried closing my eyes but the flickering was still there. I feared that this was now a permanent state. Slowly my vision returned to normality and I was left with a throbbing headache. About a week later I was in a supermarket. One of the strip lights was flashing intermittently. It caught my eye. The whole process began once more. Again, I was in a state of near panic. For months I became paranoid about lighting—waiting for the next attack. Over the years I have learned to cope with migraine. When the symptoms first occur I know what the process is going to be. It will be unpleasant but it will pass. I have learned to react appropriately. If a bout of migraine still induced that first reaction, I would be reacting inappropriately. I am sure that the fear of having another attack precipitated further attacks. We become caught up in a vicious circle.

Depression takes hold of us when we are reacting inappropriately to the events of our lives. This has a profound effect on our whole being. In his book, *Coping with Depression in the Ministry and Other Helping Professions*, Archibald D. Hart says, 'It is remarkable how even psychologically sophisticated people often overlook the following two facts: (1) We respond to what we *perceive* as happening in our environment, not to what is *actually* happening; and (2) after we have processed the perception in the light of our previous learning history, experience, biases, and so on, our minds pass the final outcome to the rest of our bodies, and the feelings of depression we then experience are the *sum* of *all* the changes in the brain as well as in the rest of the body'.[1]

# Depression and sin

B efore we go into any detail on the relationship between depression and sin, we must make some general observations. Firstly, depression is ultimately the result of sin. Depression, along with all the other ills afflicting creation, would not exist if man had not sinned. Secondly, depression can be the product of personal sin. This does not mean that depression is a sin per se, or that it is necessarily sinful to be depressed. We have already seen that there can be causes that are beyond our control. However, when we are considering the causes of depression, sin must be addressed as a crucial factor. Humanistic theories on the causes of depression ignore this at their peril!

Modern man has very little understanding of what sin is. For many it is a 'hang-up' from a bygone, unenlightened age. If there is any general concept of sin it is as some kind of wrong doing that affects the lives of other people. Anything goes, as long at it does not harm others. Secular psychologists have redefined sin in order to fit it into a philosophy that excludes moral absolutes. In his book, *Freud and Christianity*, R. S. Lee summarizes this position: 'In its simplest use the term means conduct by an individual contrary to what his conscience or moral judgement believes to be right. This view assumes that the highest good a man can do is to act according to his conscience.'[1] The origin of the conscience, and values that determine moral judgement are largely dependent on the life-history of the individual.

The Bible, however, has much to say about sin and its effect on the human race. It speaks in absolutes and is, in itself, the source book for our understanding of right and wrong.

### What is sin?

The Westminster Shorter Catechism says, 'Sin is any want of conformity unto, or transgression of, the law of God.' Two essential factors emerge from this statement. Firstly, sin is directed against God. In his great penitential Psalm, David writes, 'Against You, You only, have I sinned, And done *this* evil in Your sight—that You may be found just when You speak, *And* blameless when You judge.' (Psalm 51:4). The event that prompted

David to write these words had an adverse effect on many people (2 Samuel 11 & 12). David had seduced Bathsheba; duped and murdered her husband; implicated a faithful comrade in his crime; and brought calamity upon his family in the process. In pursuing his desires he had devastated other people's lives, yet, when brought face to face with the consequences of his actions, David knew that the worst thing he had done was to offend his God. As the apostle Paul puts it, 'For to be carnally minded is death…because the carnal mind is enmity against God'(Romans 8:6-7). However badly our sin affects others, and it does, it is only truly sin because it is directed against God himself. When the Bible speaks of sin it does so in relation to God's law. 'Whoever commits sin also commits lawlessness, and sin is lawlessness.' (1 John 3:4). Ignorance of God's law, as it is revealed in the Bible, is no excuse. For, 'when the Gentiles, who do not have the law, by nature do the things in the law, these, although not having the law, are a law to themselves, who show the work of the law written in their hearts, their conscience also bearing witness, and between themselves *their* thoughts accusing or else excusing *them*.' (Romans 2:14-15).

Sin is, ultimately, lawlessness. It is 'want of conformity unto, or transgression of, the law of God'. It is directed against God because it is disobedience to His law. We can see this by returning to the story of David and Bathsheba. We do not know the extent of Bathsheba's willingness to have a sexual relationship with the king. Maybe she was seduced by his personal charisma, or maybe she was simply afraid to do anything other than please the king. Whatever pressures David placed upon her, one thing is certain, they both disobeyed the eighth commandment, 'You shall not commit adultery'. Their relationship was an act of lawlessness. One act of lawlessness was followed by another—the murder of Uriah the Hittite. Overriding this was the failure of David to obey the first commandment, 'You shall have no other gods before me'. This act of lawlessness is at the root of all sin.

## The nature of sin
To get a true understanding of the nature of sin, so that we can accurately relate it to depression, we must look at the way in which it is described in the

Bible. This is particularly evident in the words used in the original biblical languages.

In the Old Testament, the most common word used to designate sin is *chattah* (Exodus 32:30). It expresses the idea of 'missing the mark'. It means, literally, 'a miss, misstep, or slip with the foot'. Other words are *avon* (1 Kings 17:18), which means to bend or curve, to twist, and gives the idea of the distortion which sin produces in the life of the sinner. *Pestia* (Proverbs 28:13) is often translated as 'transgression' and means just that. It refers to sin as a rebellion against God (Job 33:9; 34:6; Psalm 32:1). *Shugah* (Leviticus 4:13) speaks of sin as 'going astray'. It also refers to mistakes or to being misled.

In the New Testament, the most common word is *hamartia* (Romans 3:23). Like its Hebrew equivalent, chattah, it means to 'miss the mark'. Its use in the Hellenistic world embraced a wide range of actions, from stupidity to lawbreaking.[2] *Adika* (Acts 8:23), has the more specific meaning of unrighteousness and injustice; of wrongful character and life. *Parabasis* refers to a breach of the law (Romans 4:15), a transgression (Galatians 3:19); as does *anomia* (1 John 3:4) which effectively refers to sin as lawlessness. Other words used are, *asebia* (Titus 2:12) which denotes a sense of godlessness or irreverence towards God; and *ptaio* (James 2:10), a moral stumbling block, to trip, to make a mistake (Romans 11:11).

To summarize this we can say that as sinners we are by nature rebels against God. We do not reverence him as we ought. We fall short of the standard that he requires of us, stray from the paths that he has set before us, distort his image within us, and live in disobedience to his will.

## The effect of sin

As we have seen, sin is directed against God and is expressed in lawlessness. The Bible has much to say about the effect of sin upon the human race.

As a result of the fall, we are all inherently corrupted by it and every part of our being is polluted with it. It is part of our nature. Some people think in terms of *sins*, as if the wrong actions we take are 'out of character'. We should learn to think in terms of *sin*, whereby the actions that we take are perfectly in character. We sin because we are sinners. We are born with a corrupt nature, 'The heart is deceitful above all *things*, and desperately wicked' (Jeremiah 17:9).

As a result of this we have to live with sin's consequences. Let me refer you again to the Westminster Shorter Catechism. Q. 'What is the misery of that estate whereunto men fall?' A. 'All mankind by their fall lost communion with God, are under His wrath and curse, and so made liable to all the miseries of this life, to death itself, and to the pains of hell for ever.' Sin renders man, in his fallen state, incapable of a relationship with God (Isaiah 59:2); unable to enter his presence (Genesis 3:23); unable to do his will (John 8:34); and subject to the effect of lawlessness; God's wrath (Romans 1:18). Sin severs the relationship between God and man. We are born bereaved!

Sin also degenerates human relationships. Man replaces God with the god of the self, worshipping and serving the creature rather than the Creator. As a result, the self becomes the reference point for all our experiences. We envy others because we do not have the things that they have. Cain envied Abel and as a result murdered him (Genesis 4:1-8). As a result of sin, man exploits his fellow man in order to satisfy his own self-centredness. The Old Testament abounds with examples of such exploitation, and God's righteous anger against it. Such is the insidious nature of sin; man takes pride in his godlike status and indulges himself in self-satisfaction (Luke 12:16-21), and self-righteousness (Luke 18:9-14). As a result he judges and exploits his fellow man.

In understanding this, we cannot fail to see the import of the command, 'love your neighbour as yourself' (Mark 12:31; Leviticus 19:18). There are two ways of interpreting these words. One way would be to see these words as exhorting us to learn to love ourselves in order to love our neighbour. After all, it is argued, we cannot adequately love our neighbour if our own lives are full of inner conflict and self-loathing. We are bombarded by selfist philosophy and psychology that makes exactly this point. Sick patients need a healthy doctor. This mind set has filtered into much of present day Bible teaching and preaching. Thus, many Christians are deluded into condemning the harmful effects of selfism yet, at the same time, extolling the virtues of the philosophy that produces them.

We do not need to be taught to love ourselves; for, out of our sinful nature, self-love becomes natural. This is what the second greatest commandment means. It takes for granted that, because of sin, we are self-centred beings who love ourselves. The exhortation is to direct that same love away from self and towards our neighbour. Many may be incensed by reading these words, some may even feel hurt by what I have written, and say, 'But I do not love myself!' 'In fact, I hate myself!' 'That's always been my problem!' My reply would be, 'Why are you so concerned about yourself that you feel such an intense feeling like hatred?' May I suggest that you take a long, hard, biblical look at the way you are approaching this question of self. In a later chapter we will be doing just that. Such are the 'miseries of this life', men are encouraged to compound them by a philosophy of self-centredness.

# Death and the failure of materialism

'Vanity of vanities, all is vanity'(Ecclesiastes 1:2). These words, written in the time of Solomon, are a telling commentary on the meaninglessness of life for those soley absorbed in, and by, the material world. The fact of death ensures the failure of materialism, and presents us with a prevailing sense of impending loss if we are seeking fulfilment in this world alone. For much of the time, we can evade the issue by plunging ourselves more deeply into the cares of this world. This may work for a time but, whenever this reality is brought home to us, it will inevitably have a deeply depressing effect.

## The fact of death

The most obvious effect of sin upon man is death (Romans 6:23). No amount of denial of the universality and power of sin can nullify its consequence. We all die. This was made clear to our first parents (Genesis 2:17). As a result of their lawlessness the inevitable fact was produced in their bodies (Genesis 3:19), and transmitted to every generation, 'Therefore, just as through one man sin entered into the world, and death through sin, and thus death spread to all men, because all sinned' (Romans 5:12). As Bruce Milne puts it, 'We are given time by God, but it moves inexorably to its close, when all our plans, purposes and dreams are finally bracketed by mortality.'[1]

As the ultimate consequence of sin, physical death, *death in time*, leads on to spiritual death, *death in eternity*. 'And as it is appointed for men to die once, but after that the judgement'(Hebrews 9:27). Nothing is more awesome for man than to face the inevitable judgement of God upon sin. As a result of sin, unregenerate man must face the eternal reality of hell.

Man was not created to die. Death has come upon us because of sin (Genesis 2:17; Romans 5:12). The term 'natural causes' is often used to refer to the means which caused a person's death. This is true from the perspective of fallen humanity, but not true in the sense in which man has been created.

Death is not natural. As Louis Berkhof puts it, 'Death is not represented as something natural to the life of man, a mere falling short of an ideal, but very decidedly foreign and hostile to human life.'[2] Man may endeavour to accept death stoically, and to bow to its inevitability, but at the heart of his thinking he knows that he was created for life and that death is not truly part of the natural order of things. Death is truly a curse on fallen humanity (Galatians 3:13). The great Puritan writer, Thomas Watson, described the miseries which sin has produced in man as, 'the sour core in the apple which our first parents ate'. He goes on to say, 'There had never been a stone in the kidneys, if there had not been first a stone in the heart. Yea, the death of the body is the fruit and result of original sin. . . Adam was made immortal, conditionally, if he had not sinned. Sin dug Adam's grave. Death is terrible to nature.'[3]

Death, however, is not just an event at the end of the life-chain. It is something that we carry around with us in our bodies and our minds. We see the passing years etched on our faces. We face the inevitable decline of our physical strength. We are continually aware that, through disease or accident the process of life can come to an abrupt halt. We know that we can die today.

Death is a taboo subject. As a rule, most people do not even want to think about it. It is not a popular topic of conversation at a dinner party or even a church social. A number of people I know are reluctant to make their last will and testament because they find it uncomfortable contemplating their own death. It is thought impolite to bring the subject of death into a conversation. Man tries his best to push the fact to the back of his mind and is largely quite successful in doing this, but the circumstances of life push it to the forefront of his thinking.

In our minds, death has its consequences. Firstly—*fear*. Fear of an unknown experience that takes us out of conscious relationship with the material world that has been our home. Fear of annihilation—that we will never be conscious of anything again. Secondly—*loss*. Death ends everything. All that we have achieved and striven for in our lives is lost. Along the way, death snatches our loved ones from us. Thirdly—*futility*. Because of death life seems futile. It would have been better if we had not had a taste of consciousness at all. In the end, everything is meaningless. These factors underline the unnaturalness of death, thus making it man's greatest foe.

## The failure of materialism

We also see the effect of sin in the failure of materialism. Man, because of sin, cannot enter into a spiritual relationship with God. Therefore, he turns to the tangible things of this world in order to find a meaning and purpose for his life. Although such things bring temporal satisfaction, they soon lose their initial importance and man moves on to something else—never quite possessing enough, achieving enough, or receiving enough. The Bible speaks clearly about the futility of such a pursuit. It was evident in the teaching of Jesus, 'For what profit is it to a man if he gains the whole world, and loses his own soul?' (Matthew 16:26). 'But take heed to yourselves, lest your hearts be weighed down with carousing, drunkenness, and cares of this life, and that Day come on you unexpectedly.' (Luke 21:34). The author of the book of Ecclesiastes clearly shows the emptiness of materialism, 'He who loves silver will not be satisfied with silver; Nor he who loves abundance with increase. This also is vanity. When goods increase, They increase who eat them; So what profit have the owners except to see *them* with their eyes?' (Ecclesiastes 5:10-11).

Why is this the case? It is because man has been created as a spiritual being, to love and to serve God. Sin has turned his heart from God to the world. The world is only a temporary dwelling and so man is racing against time to make something of a fleeting life—pursuing things that can never truly be his because both they and he are passing away. Everything material is vulnerable. Nothing on this earth will ever be ours. Either we will lose it along the way or we will leave it behind. The Bible sums it up powerfully for us, 'Therefore I hated life because the work that was done under the sun is grievous to me, for all is vanity and grasping for the wind. Then I hated all my labour in which I had toiled under the sun, because I must leave it to the man who comes after me'(Ecclesiastes 2:17-18). If this world brought fulfilment and satisfaction, the rich and famous would rarely be depressed! Yet, even recent history is littered with accounts of alcoholism, drug abuse, and even suicide among the 'successful' people of our day.

The advancing years of our lives bring this truth home to us. When we are young the quest for advancement in the material things of this world is filled with excitement. We are taught to plan and prepare for the future at an increasingly earlier age. Education is paramount—then on to a career, a spouse, children, house, pension.... and then? Of course, all these things are legitimate pursuits. We live in a material world and have to make the necessary provision. The danger is that these things become an end in themselves. When we reach middle age things begin to change, sometimes dramatically. The extent whether we have succeeded or failed in our material quest becomes irrelevant. In moments of reflection we conclude that we have fallen short of the ideal that was fixed in our minds at the very beginning. Our lives have not turned out as we have imagined. Most of us have underachieved and the few who would be considered successful have found their success to be an anticlimax. Why is this so? Simply because, without God, we have been pursuing a hopeless ideal of fulfilment that cannot be realized solely in human achievement.

One of the most influential psychiatrists of the twentieth century, Carl Gustav Jung, saw this clearly. Man, according to Jung, possesses a 'natural religious function'. He noted the increasing tendency towards depression in men over forty and women over thirty-five. This, he concluded, was a turning point in life and was primarily the result of the failure to find and fulfil this religious function. Jung's religious theories are far removed from evangelical Christianity, yet he hit upon an important truth. Unless a man experiences 'God' in his own being and finds the expression of that experience within his 'religion', he will become psychologically fragmented, neurotic, often depressed. The god of Jung's psychological/religious theories was ultimately the self. The pursuit of religious experience was centred on the process of self-realisation and fulfilment, which Jung called 'individuation'. Jung saw that man had an inbuilt propensity to look beyond the material. Man's libidinal drive was primarily spiritual. This contributes to our understanding of why, in the most materialistic of societies, people seek some kind of expression of spirituality through the New Age religions and their paraphernalia. Man is seeking to express his 'natural religious function' in a state of sin. Blinded by the god of this world he has rejected the truth revealed to him in the Bible, yet he cannot deny the God given capacity for spiritual knowledge. This contributes to a deep sense of unease and despair about his life and his destiny. This leads naturally on to the next object of our attention.

# Depression and conviction of sin

We have already seen that at the root of sin is lawlessness. Hovering over man is the judgement of God resulting from this. Buried deep within the heart of man is the knowledge that this judgement will inevitably take place. We cannot plead ignorance, for God has made it perfectly clear through 'the work of the law written in their hearts' (Romans 2:15). In other words—the *conscience*. We will examine the nature and role of the conscience in greater detail in later chapters, but here we need to make some general observations.

Firstly, what is the conscience? Speaking of all men, the Bible says, 'Their conscience also bearing witness, and between themselves *their* thoughts accusing or else *excusing* them.' (Romans 2:15). The word *conscience* is a translation of the Greek, *suneidesis*. Its root, *suneido* means, 'to see completely or to understand'. It is used in relation to morality—the knowledge of right and wrong. Thayer speaks of it as the soul 'distinguishing between what is morally good and bad, prompting to do the former and shun the latter, commanding the one and condemning the other'. The conscience is an 'inner witness'; something that does not operate solely from the desire of the self to do its own will. *Suneido* gives a clear picture of the conscience as being co-perceptive. It is, in a sense, like having another person within us, checking the sometimes excessive demands of the self.

Secondly, how does it work? Its source is God. It is an operation of common grace upon all men. It does not just regulate behaviour or attitude. It convicts men of the truth of their Creator and their guilt of lawlessness in his sight. In the first two chapters of Romans, the apostle Paul demolishes any ideas that man has no knowledge of such truth. God's anger is revealed to men (Romans 1:19); the creation itself testifies to his 'eternal power and Godhead'(Romans 1:19-20); man has 'exchanged the truth of God for a lie'(Romans 1:25); man has rejected God (Romans 1:21); committed idolatry (Romans 1:22-23) and subsequently been consumed by his own lusts (Romans 1:24-31). Man has even hardened his heart against God (Romans 1:32). Man is without excuse and knows it (Romans 2:1-9). How does he know it? Through conscience (Romans 2:15).

Man's attempts to deal with this graphically show the deceitfulness of the human heart. 'Therefore you are inexcusable, O man, whoever you are who judge, for in whatever you judge another you condemn yourself: For you who judge practice the same things.' (Romans 2:1). Man has no righteousness of his own, so he seeks to produce it through judgementalism. He tries to salve his conscience by creating a diversion. Why do we find it so easy to find fault with others? Why is it that tabloid editors have discovered that stories denigrating and destroying public figures sells newspapers? When we talk about someone, do we tend to extol their virtues or publish their vices? We can live under the mistaken notion that by finding fault with others we will somehow feel better about ourselves. As we are incapable of raising ourselves up, we may be tempted to do the next best thing by putting others down. Not only is this futile, and damaging to those who are on the receiving end, it is an affront to Almighty God, who sees through our pathetic attempts to override the conscience in this way. Jesus loudly condemned such behaviour, 'Judge not, that you be not judged. For with what judgement you judge, you will be judged; and with the same measure you use, it will be measured back to you.' (Matthew 7:1-2). What angered the Son of God most during His earthly ministry? Surely it was the sin of self righteousness? What was at the root of this? Surely it was the denial of the truth of man's lawlessness? This was especially pertinent to the Pharisees, who had the law. However, through the operation of the God given conscience, no man has an excuse!

What has this to do with depression? The answer is quite clear. The conscience is a God given means by which we can evaluate our attitudes and actions. It monitors and regulates our lives. When we do what is right our consciences are clear. When we choose the wrong our consciences are troubled. To cope with his sinful estate, man has developed the capacity to deaden or dull his conscience so that it does not trouble him excessively. This varies from individual to individual, from the scrupulous neurotic to the psychopath. Most of us are somewhere in between. In rejecting God, his law, and ultimately his Son, Jesus Christ, man flies in the face of his own conscience. Let us take the example of the British people. As a general rule, we have cast aside the Christian influence of our history. We have relegated the Christian faith to one of many ways to God. We have rejected the Bible and its moral teaching; desecrated the Sabbath; and taught our children Selfism in place of the gospel. We have done away with moral absolutes. Everything is relative and subservient to the pursuit of self gratification and fulfilment. Humanistic philosophy and psychology have removed sin and replaced it with 'sickness'. By throwing away the Bible and rewriting the rules, man thinks that he has expunged the law, and ultimately its judgement, but all he has done is to have 'exchanged the truth of God for the lie'. (Romans 1:25).

Human beings are resourceful. In most cases, the dulled conscience does not trouble us too much, but there are, and always will be, times when the circumstances of life sharpen them and bring us face to face with the truth that is written by God on our hearts. I often think of this when I am conducting a funeral and look out at the sea of faces in the congregation. Face to face with the reality of death there is nowhere to run and hide. Those closest to the deceased are consumed with grief, but there are those who are on the fringe, the neighbour, the representative from the company, or the distant cousin who are not quite sure how to handle the occasion. Body language makes it clear that some are desperately trying to switch off—to divert their minds from the awful truth that lies before them. Overheard conversations after the service, confirm that every attempt is being made to assuage even the remotest feeling that consciences are being pricked and mortality is being brought to mind. The life events that bring us stress often reveal the cracks that have been papered over with the pursuits of the world. The conscience is laid bare and must be repapered over as quickly as possible. Is it any wonder that we live in an age and a society where depression is rampant?

## Conviction, conversion and depression
Someone has said, 'Neurotics build castles in the air, psychotics live in them, and psychiatrists collect the rent.' In describing the process of conviction and conversion, I am tempted to add, 'and Jesus Christ demolishes them and builds a road through to the kingdom of God.' Of

course, it ruins the joke, but I am not trying to make light of the pain of mental affliction. The important point being made here is that in some cases the cause of a person's depression may not be physical or psychological, but spiritual namely, conviction of sin.

In the upper room, the Lord Jesus Christ taught his disciples that after he had died, risen, and ascended, he would send the Holy Spirit to them. Speaking of the Spirit's work, he said, 'And when He has come, He will convict the world of sin, and of righteousness, and of judgement: of sin, because they do not believe in Me; of righteousness, because I go to my Father and you see me no more; of judgement, because the ruler of this world is judged.' (John 16:8-11).

We have already looked at the role of the conscience in natural man. We must now examine the crucial work of the Holy Spirit in bringing men and women to Christ. When discussing the causes and cures for depression this factor is wholly ignored by secular theorists. Yet it is a crucial issue and must be addressed.

In an earlier chapter we related some experiences of how people felt when they were depressed. Let me relate another one. In my early twenties I started to get nagging thoughts about my mortality. I was young, healthy, and had just begun a new business venture that was going to set me up for life. Everything on the surface was fine, but underneath there was an occasional feeling of pointlessness to it all. The occasions for such feelings began to increase. I soon began to develop symptoms that we associate with depression. My life felt empty, even though I was busy seeking to build a business. I could not sleep at night and did not want to get up in the morning. I had little energy or desire for work, even though I was going through the motions. Everything seemed grey and pointless. I began to drink heavily to blot out the feeling of despair, not realising that alcohol is a depressant and not an anti-depressant! Things came to a head when on a business trip I spent an entire night looking out of a hotel window, unable to take my eyes off a solitary tree being lashed by the wind. It looked old and battered, and I wondered how many had looked at the same tree from the same window. Where were they now? Some of them would surely be dead and gone. Others would have got on with their lives, but to what purpose? I remembered some words that I had read somewhere, 'vanity of vanities, all is vanity.' I knew that I could not go on feeling like this and had to find some way out of my condition. When I returned home, I started to read my grandfather's Bible. He had been a preacher, and his own notes and comments were scattered through its pages. I have to say that, at the time, the Bible did not seem to help that much. I did not know where to look for help and did not understand what I was reading. Two things, however, kept me going. Firstly, there was something about the book that made me feel that I was on the right track. Secondly, it was obvious from my grandfather's notes that he believed it to be the Word of God, and I felt that if he had found the answer, I would, too. I started to go to church on a Sunday evening and listen to the faithful preaching of the gospel. The preaching made me feel even more depressed about my condition, but the fact that I was surrounded by people who obviously had found meaning and purpose in their lives comforted me so much that I continued to go. Although I still felt trapped in my depressed condition I noticed a shift in my attitude. I no longer believed that life itself was meaningless, I now believed that *my* life was meaningless. I realized that I was responsible for my condition. This made me feel worse but it also made me feel better. It made me feel worse because it brought home to me the helplessness of my state. It made me feel better because it brought with it the remote possibility that somewhere in the darkness there was a light, and maybe, one day it would shine on me. Slowly dawn broke. I realized that God had sent His Son into this world for people like me, to crash into the darkness and rescue us from our helpless condition. It was my sin that had separated me from God and Jesus Christ had atoned for that sin. With much struggle I eventually surrendered to God's truth and cast myself upon His mercy. The joy and relief were inexpressible. During this whole period I did not feel any inclination to seek medical or psychological help.

I use my own personal testimony, not just because I like talking about myself, but to emphasize an important point. Christian biography abounds with such stories of what appears to be depression preceding conversion. We have only to read the accounts of the lives of people like John Bunyan, John Wesley, Jonathan Edwards, C. H. Spurgeon and countless others to realize that this is so. However, there is a great danger that, by reading such accounts, we have the misguided notion that these are exceptional experiences for exceptional people! I use my own account to emphasize that this was not an exceptional experience, and that I am certainly not an exceptional person. People who know me well will confirm this!

It is clear from the scriptural way of salvation that conviction of sin is an essential part of true conversion to Christ. The way in which this manifests itself in the individual is unique. For some it will indeed be a 'dark night of the soul', but for others it may be less intense and debilitating. Nevertheless, whatever our perception of what is happening to us, God the Holy Spirit is at work. Salvation is God's work of sovereign grace in us. We cannot thwart His purpose. However, if we treat depressive symptoms solely on a medical/psychological basis, are we not in danger of quenching the Holy Spirit's work in salvation?

The subject of conviction of sin can create a major problem for many who consider themselves to be Christians. Aware of a need for fulfilment, a person may be urged to come to Jesus Christ, the one who will meet all his need. After completing a course of instruction, or having an ecstatic experience at a meeting, he may be encouraged to make a commitment to Christ and assured that by doing this he will be born again into a new life with God. This involves an acknowledgement of sin but with little understanding of its meaning and consequences. Having sincerely made his commitment, the new 'believer' enthusiastically involves himself in the life of the church. Everything is going well. God is blessing him and he thrives in the warm fellowship of his fellow Christians. Then, sometime later, he begins to feel a sense of emptiness returning to his life. He starts to feel depressed. His friends tell him that Christians do not get depressed, it is the devil attacking his faith. Satan is rebuked, but he still feels depressed. Is he suffering from depression, caused by physical or psychological factors? Possibly. But there is another possibility. He is experiencing something that should have happened at the very beginning; something not adequately dealt with by a 'gospel' that makes light of sin. He is undergoing conviction of sin and the true process of conversion. He does not need to rebuke the devil or seek medical help. He needs to come to God the biblical way, in true repentance and faith.

We have seen, in this chapter, the effect of sin and its relationship to depression, from its general effect on man and his environment, to the specific work of conviction by the Holy Spirit. Whenever we turn our attention to the subject of depression we must address and deal with these great factors.

# Depression and guilt

We all experience feelings of guilt. These may be the result of something we have said or left unsaid; an action that cannot be put right; an event that can never be erased from the memory; or a relationship that did not work. We also know that there may be those who will try to make us feel guilty in order to manipulate us or ensure our continual devotion. Sometimes an aged parent, a demanding spouse, or a spoilt child may try to manipulate us in this way. We often carry the burden of guilt around with us until it becomes too heavy to bear and we collapse beneath its load into depression. The people who need us most no longer receive the care and attention they deserve. We even begin to feel guilty about feeling guilty! Is there a way out of this trap? There is, if we approach the question of guilt in a sensible and sensitive way.

When we are depressed, guilt-feelings tend to intensify. We are usually physically exhausted, and become hypersensitive to our sins, faults and failings. Depression is invariably accompanied by anxiety, and our feelings of anxiety reinforce our guilt feelings. Sometimes we feel that our depression is the result of our own sin—a kind of punishment inflicted upon us. Most of the time we feel guilty about being depressed, especially when we see the effect it has on those around us.

These feelings of guilt must be challenged. For a person to be pronounced 'guilty' in a court of law there has to be evidence that a crime has been committed, and that the person charged is responsible for committing it. A depressed person often feels like the prisoner in the dock. The conscience is the prosecuting counsel; the evidence of guilt is overwhelming; the defence counsel is silent; the 'guilty' verdict is inevitable. When we are depressed, we are too tired to defend ourselves against inner accusations of guilt. This chapter, in a sense, is our defence counsel, challenging the evidence against us. Quite rightly, there are times when we will be advised to plead 'guilty' and throw ourselves upon the mercy of the court! Often, there will be no case to answer and we will be set free from the charges brought against us!

Legal criteria must be used when challenging our feelings of guilt. Is there any evidence to support this feeling of guilt? The evidence is substantiated by the authenticity and accuracy of its source.

## Guilt and guilt-feelings

Guilt is essentially a legal issue; and guilt-feelings a moral one. Ideally, someone who *is* guilty should *feel* guilty; and, someone who *feels* guilty should actually *be* guilty. Sadly, this is not always the case; hence the need for this chapter. Guilt and guilt-feelings do not always coincide. Perpetrators of great crimes often show little or no remorse for their actions, while some people are in a constant state of 'guilt' over things for which they bear no responsibility.

Guilt is a God-given instrument for determining and directing our well-being. We feel guilty when we think or act in a way that contradicts what we believe to be right. The Bible teaches that the moral standards that determine our guilt are provided by a holy and just God. These, however, are shaped and supplemented by other factors. This is why we must never trust our guilt-feelings alone. Some of the things that make us feel guilty are due to teaching we received in childhood that has no bearing whatsoever on biblical truth. These things, however, have become so rooted in our consciousness, that we treat them as if they were written on tablets of stone.

A sense of guilt serves an essential purpose in the life and growth of a person. It leads us to reconciliation with God, and with others, and enables us to make peace within ourselves. If we do not feel guilty we will never accept responsibility for our wrong doing. Guilt also enables us to live in a society where accepted morality is the norm.

What makes us feel guilty? The answer should be simple but, because of the sinful nature of the human heart, it has become complex. The true origin of guilt is to be found in God alone. He has given us his Word (Hebrews 4:12); his own presence in the person of the Holy Spirit (John 16:8), and implanted a conscience in each one of us (Romans 2:15). This should be the sole source of guilt. Sin is the transgression of his law; guilt is the fact of our personal responsibility in the matter, 'For whoever shall keep the whole law, and yet stumble in one *point*, he is guilty of all.' (James 2:10).

When dealing with guilt and guilt feelings we must also take into account the world, the flesh, and the devil. The world, because we are influenced by the standards of the society in which we live. The flesh, because our consciences are affected by our past experiences. The devil, because Satan is the arch-deceiver and will always seek to pervert truth in order to lead us into bondage.

Guilt-feelings must always be challenged to establish the authenticity of their source. When I was a boy we used to supplement our pocket-money by collecting empty bottles from friends and neighbours and taking them to the local shop to collect the deposits. We would generally arrive with three or four large bags or boxes full of assorted bottles. They were heavy, but the anticipation of the riches that would soon be ours seemed to give added strength to our young limbs. Our entrepreneurial adventures always ended in disappointment. We never seemed to learn. However persistent we were, the shop-keeper would only accept bottles that he had originally sold. We made our weary way home with just a few pence, wondering how we were going to get rid of all the bottles we were carrying around with us!

Genuine guilt is like the bottle that is rightfully ours and on which we must pay back the deposit. Guilt-feelings, that do not originate in genuine guilt, are like the bottles that have been passed on to us by others, and which we carry around wondering what we are going to do with them.

Christians tend to accept guilt readily. We would never have come to Christ if this were not the case. However, we can become the dumping ground for other people's guilt. By accepting this we harm ourselves and, in the long term, do no favours for the person who is trying to make us feel guilty. We, in effect, distort something that God has given us for our well-being.

## The purpose of guilt

'The act of sin passeth away, but the guilt abideth on the person, and must do until the law be satisfied, and the sinner thereon absolved. This naturally produceth fear, which is the first expression of a sense of guilt.'[1] So wrote the great seventeenth century theologian, John Owen. In these few words, Owen encapsulates much of what we need to know about guilt and its purpose and effect upon our lives. Guilt is the product of sin. A sinful act soon passes into history, but the guilt remains. Notice two phrases that Owen uses; 'guilt abideth on a person' and 'a sense of guilt'. Here we see the true nature of guilt and guilt-feelings. Firstly, he speaks of the fact of guilt; the culpability we bear for our sin. It 'abideth' on us; it is ours, and we must carry it around until we find some way of dealing with it. Secondly, he speaks of the effect of guilt; the emotion that it produces within us; namely, fear. The fear induced by guilt may express itself in a number of ways. We may be afraid of the consequences of our action; the harm that it has done to others. Alternatively, we may simply be afraid of being found out and the shame that will inevitably follow. We should, however, be concerned for the judgement that will surely be meted out on us as the consequence of our guilt.

Owen also makes another important point. Our guilt, and the fear that it produces, will always be with us until it is satisfactorily dealt with. This can only be done when the law is satisfied and the sinner absolved. The law can only be satisfied when its judgement is meted out upon our sin; we can only be absolved when that judgement is completed. The Bible makes it abundantly clear what the nature of that judgement is, 'For the wages of sin *is* death'(Romans 6:23). The same passage goes on to say, 'but the gift of God *is* eternal life in Christ Jesus our Lord.' This is the purpose of the atoning death and resurrection of Christ; the law is satisfied and the sinner absolved (2 Corinthians 5:21; Hebrews 10:22).

Here is the positive nature of guilt. We are to acknowledge and confess our sins, knowing that they have been dealt with on the legal basis of Christ's death (1 John 1:9-10). We are, wherever possible, to put right the wrongs we have committed against others (Matthew 5:21-24). We are to resolve to sin no more (John 8:10-11). The effect of this is not just legal. It is also psychological. As the guilt is removed, so should the fear that accompanies it. Here is all we need to know about the purpose of guilt, yet, as we have already discovered, the sinful nature of man has so distorted our understanding of the subject, we are left with a residue of guilt and guilt-feelings that do not seem to belong with us. We now need to look at the origin of this confusion and the way that we can sort out the wheat from the chaff.

## Accepting or denying

As we learn to differentiate between true guilt and guilt-feelings, we must go on to the stage where we accept the guilt that is rightfully ours, and reject guilt feelings that have no substance in truth. Before we do this, we must make an honest character assessment. We must decide whether we are, by nature, someone who readily accepts guilt, or usually denies it. The acceptor tends to take responsibility for all guilt feelings whatever their origin. He is someone who feels responsible for everyone else's happiness and well-being. The denier does not even accept genuine guilt. Always blaming someone else, he will have a plausible excuse for his actions. By off-loading his guilt onto another person, he will feel able to carry on with life as if nothing has happened. We see this illustrated in some marriages, where one spouse seems to take the blame for everything that goes wrong.

Both states are unhealthy and unholy. The acceptor is overburdened with a sense of guilt that is impossible to bear—only Christ is qualified or able to bear the guilt of another. The denier may well feel a temporary sense of relief, but the guilt will remain until properly dealt with. The acceptor may become depressed because he is overburdened with a sense of guilt that prevents him from functioning properly. The denier may become depressed, because he at last feels guilty and does not know what to do about it.

Guilt is moral pain. Pain tells us that something is wrong. We can deal with it in a number of ways. We can deny it until it gets so bad that we must do something about it. We can take painkillers and cover it up so that it does not trouble us. The right course of action is to find out its cause as soon as possible. If it is something inside us we must try to put it right. If, on the other hand, it is caused by someone else, we must not allow them to do this to us. Would you just sit still and let someone deliberately hurt you?

## Dealing with guilt-feelings

Guilt-feelings are not easy to deal with, especially if we have lived with them for a number of years. They can, and must, be dealt with in order to heal the depression that may have resulted from them. If we are prepared to approach the problem boldly and honestly, we can expect a remarkable change in our sense of well-being and our relationships with others, not to mention our relationship with God! I would suggest the following procedure:

1. Recognize that feeling guilty is normal. Only psychopaths never feel guilty.

2. Check the source of your guilt-feeling. Is it based on biblical truth?

3. Make an honest list of the things you feel guilty about. Do not be afraid to take advice from a trusted Christian friend or counsellor.

4. Divide your list into three categories: genuine guilt; guilt-feelings that have no source in truth; and the one's you are not sure about.

5. Acknowledge true guilt. Ask God's forgiveness. If possible, put right any wrongs. If this is not possible, leave it there. You can do no more. The key is to do everything you can.

6. Refuse any guilt that is not yours. Acceptance is often no more than a bad habit. We cannot carry other people's guilt for them. We are not helping them by doing so; we are simply denying them the route to their own reconciliation with God and to their health and well-being. When someone, either past or present, tries to make you feel unnecessarily guilty, do not allow them to do so.

7. When you are unsure about a guilt-feeling, ask God for guidance. Look at it in the light of your present understanding of the Bible. Seek more knowledge. Do not accept it or reject it until you are sure of its source. When I feel guilty my instinct is to accept responsibility. If, after honestly looking at the origin of a guilt-feeling in the light of Scripture, I am still not sure, I take it to God in confession, knowing that he will forgive me. At this point, I get an inkling if the guilt is really mine. If I believe that I am responsible, I try to do all I can to put it right. If I still feel guilty, then I know that my guilt-feeling does not originate in truth, so I refuse to accept it, dwell on it, confess it or do anything else with it.

# The origin of guilt-feelings

The Bible teaches that God declares man guilty of breaking his law. 'You shall not take the name of the Lord your God in vain, for the Lord will not hold *him* guiltless who takes His name in vain'(Exodus 20:7). In order to bring about the process of reconciliation, God convicts his people of their guilt. They are made to *feel* guilty. This is illustrated in the story of the prodigal son who 'came to himself' when he realized the consequences of his sin (Luke 15:17). Guilt-feelings, that originate in God's desire to bring his people to repentance and faith are specific. David was deeply convicted of his sin through his relationship with Bathsheba (2 Samuel 11&12); the prophets of the Old Testament laid specific charges at the feet of God's people (Hosea 4; Amos 2); Jesus was specific in his charges against the Pharisees (Luke 11:27-54); in the New Testament church the Holy Spirit convicted specifically (Acts 5). God does not give his people vague guilt feelings. When he convicts us of sin he hits the nail squarely on the head.

There are a number of words used in the New Testament that refer to guilt. They give an accurate, overall picture of the right attitude we must adopt in dealing with guilt and guilt feelings. The word *enochos* is a frequently used legal term for liability. This would coincide with the way in which we generally use the word 'guilt'. It speaks of someone who is bound, under obligation, and liable to punishment or penalty. It occurs three times in Jesus' discourse on the true nature of murder: 'But I say to you that whoever is angry with his brother without cause shall be in *danger of the judgement*. And whoever says to his brother , 'Raca!' shall be in *danger of the council*. But whoever says, 'You fool!' shall be in *danger of hell fire*'(Matthew 5:22) [Italics mine]. Paul uses the word in reference to one participating in the Lord's Supper in an unworthy manner, who will be 'guilty of the body and blood of the Lord'(1 Corinthians 11:27); and James, in terms of being guilty of the whole law if we stumble in just one point (James 2:10). It is used at the trial of Jesus, when he was considered as 'deserving of death'(Matthew 26:66; Mark 14:64).

*Aitia* speaks of the evidence itself—the cause or reason for the legal guilt.

It will be helpful to trace its usage in the trials of the apostle Paul. After a commotion in Jerusalem, Paul is arrested and brought before the Roman commander so that 'he should be examined under scourging, so that he might know why they shouted so against him'(Acts 22:24). Paul is sent to appear before Felix, governor of Caesarea. In a letter, the commander explains his actions saying, 'I wanted to know why they were accusing him'(Acts 23:28). Paul vigorously maintains his innocence before Felix, and after a period of two years of incarceration appears before Festus and Agrippa. Paul denies his guilt saying, 'For if I am an offender, or I have committed anything deserving of death, I do not object to dying; but if there is nothing in these things of which these men accuse me, no one can deliver me to them. I appeal to Caesar.'(Acts 25:11). There was no concrete evidence to bring before the court (Acts 25:18). Festus brings Paul before Agrippa in order to find some valid charge with which to send him to Rome, 'For it seems to me unreasonable to send a prisoner and not specify the charges against him.'(Acts 25:27). The purpose of highlighting this passage is to emphasize a biblical principle concerning guilt. In the Scriptures, guilt is always accompanied by a cause or reason. This provides us with a touchstone on which to test our guilt-feelings. It is essential that we learn to think biblically about our guilt-feelings. This brings us on to our next word, *elencho.*

Whereas *enochos* speaks of liability; and *aitia* of the cause or reason for liability; *elencho* refers to conviction. It signifies something that is proved and tested, exposed, or brought to light. True guilt convicts us (I Corinthians 14:24), and rebukes us (1 Timothy 5:20). This is the immediate aspect of guilt that man shuns the most, for it is accompanied by shame, 'For everyone practising evil hates the light and does not come to the light, lest his deeds should be exposed.'(John 3:20). Speaking of the work of the Holy Spirit, Jesus says, 'And when He has come, He will convict the world of sin, and of righteousness, and of judgement'. (John 16:8). Whoever walks in the light of God's truth will come under conviction of sin and feel guilty. Knowing that the purpose of such conviction is to bring him to repentance and faith, and reconciliation to the God whom he has offended, he will accept his guilt and readily accept God's mercy. True guilt is *constructive,* and not *destructive.* Why then, do Christians have so many problems with guilt? A look at the psychological theories on guilt may throw some light on the subject.

The key area is the conscience. We have already come to a biblical understanding of the role of the conscience, but we have to acknowledge that there are other, non-biblical, factors that are instrumental in guilt. The psychiatrist, Gaius Davies, highlights three problems with the conscience.[1] Firstly, *unjust condemnation*. This, as he points out, is common, 'when depression settles like a black cloud and we may feel we will never be happy again.' A person in such a condition feels that there is no way out—no forgiveness—no absolution. Secondly, *loss of conscience*. The person who 'appears to have mislaid his conscience.' The extreme example of this would be the 'psychopath', who commits heinous crimes with no feelings of remorse. Most people, however, have blind spots in their consciences, where the conscience has been dulled and desensitized in one particular area; where a certain sin or sinful personality trait is acceptable. Thirdly, *excessive scrupulosity*, or an obsessive desire for perfection. This manifests itself in excessive cleanliness or tidiness; obsessive preoccupation with time-keeping, and many other things. These are all areas where failure to meet the standard results in guilt-feelings.

While accepting guilt in its legal and moral sense, many psychologists see guilt-feelings as primarily destructive rather than constructive. Some go as far as to blame religion for this state of affairs. In examining some of the theories, we must bear in mind that the humanistic psychologist does not recognize absolute truth as it is revealed in the Bible. He does not have a theology of guilt; therefore he must look for other origins or causes for the condition.

The psychologist, Arthur Reber defines guilt as, 'an emotional state produced by the knowledge that one has violated moral standards.' He goes on to say that, 'most authorities recognize an emotional state as guilt only when the individual has internalized the moral standards of the society; thus it is distinguished from simple fear of punishment from external sources—guilt is, in a sense, a self-administered punishment.'[2] The key, for the psychologist, is the internalization of moral standards. The source of guilt is to be found in the moral standards that have been imprinted upon the personality of the individual. There are a number of theories that we shall examine.

Before we proceed any further we must address an important issue. Humanistic theories reject the Bible's teaching on guilt. Therefore, the Christian must proceed with great caution and examine all such theories in the light of Scripture. The humanist seeks to denigrate and ultimately destroy truth as it is revealed to us in the Scriptures. He sees sin as a sickness, and in rejecting biblical teaching on sin he rejects the true nature of guilt. I remember counselling a young woman who was suffering emotional anguish. After a few weeks, I discovered that we met on the same day as her appointments with her psychiatrist. The biblical teaching she was receiving in the morning was being dismissed as 'superstitious rubbish' in the afternoon! I hasten to add that not all psychiatrists are as arrogant and insensitive as this one! We must acknowledge, however, that not all guilt feelings are related to actual guilt. We have already learned that it is crucial for us to differentiate between the guilt that is truly ours and other strong emotions that masquerade as true guilt. Humanistic psychology, in its quest for the origin of guilt feelings, gives us food for thought when we unravel another knot in the tangled chain, 'Why do I feel guilty when there is no reason?'

The key areas highlighted by psychologists in the area of guilt's origin are; infancy, parental influence, learned behaviour and social pressures.

There are many theories as to how our infant experiences shape our ideas of guilt and introduce guilt feelings. Many psychologists adopt the theory that one of the earliest emotions we feel is anxiety, and that anxiety feelings cannot be adequately expressed until self-consciousness is developed. Without the emergence of self-consciousness, these anxiety feelings are expressed in a form of guilt. As John McKenzie puts it, 'For a true sense of guilt feelings we have to wait for the growth of the conscience; it is then that the real moral element is experienced. That undoubtedly begins with self-consciousness.'[3] Freud expounded theories of the Oedepus complex; the development of the super ego; and the ego ideal. Whether these are helpful or not is debatable. Some of our guilt-feelings may originate in infancy, but the how's and when's of the matter are open to question. The danger of speculating in this area is that we can easily be swayed into thinking that most of the problems we experience in adult life are not our fault, but stem from the earliest experiences, even those within the womb! This can cause great problems when we attempt to deal with present guilt feelings. Although some psychologists feel that this theory fully explains the origin of guilt-feelings, we are still left struggling to find an adequate explanation for the fully formed adult conscience.

Parental influence is crucial to the development of the adult conscience. The Bible clearly shows parental responsibility in this matter (Deuteronomy 4:9; 6:7). What we are taught and what we observe in our parents' behaviour have a lasting effect upon our lives and contribute greatly to our guilt-feelings well into adulthood. It is a tragedy that much of psychology's obsession with our relationship with our parents seems to encourage us to blame them for our present condition. Intentionally or unintentionally, many psychological theories have undermined the God-given authority of parents and seriously challenged the seventh commandment, 'Honour your father and your mother.' (Exodus 20:12). We must adopt a respectfully balanced view of the role of our parents in the development of our consciences. They are sinners just like us. They made mistakes, which we should challenge and not perpetuate. Some of the things they taught us were wrong; many of their examples were misleading. However, they did their best, as we do ours, and they must not be blamed for the present state of our lives. God holds *us* responsible for our condition, whatever the factors that go to make up that present condition.

Parental influence overlaps into a wider issue of learned behaviour. Behavioural psychology accounts for the development of the conscience in terms of learned behaviour that has been either rewarded or punished. This begins in our home life and is supplemented in our experiences at school and elsewhere. Certain kinds of behaviour are rewarded and others punished. What we are taught affects our attitude towards right and wrong. Biblical truth is either re-affirmed or contradicted. Sometimes biblical truth is distorted. In the Sermon on the Mount (Matthew 5-7), Jesus has to deal with this problem of learned behaviour among the people. He is correcting distorted teaching that masquerades as truth. What had been written in the law had been 'interpreted' and passed on as the law itself. We have to accept that some of the 'truth' that is embedded in our consciences and contributes in the production of guilt-feelings has been distorted in the same way. The problem that kept the church in theological darkness until the advent of the reformation and publication of the Bible in the common tongue, is similar to the problem that still keeps many Christians in psychological darkness today! The Bible is the source book for our understanding of true guilt.

# Depression and the Christian life (1)

The Christian life presents its own unique problems; problems, we must say, that are vastly outweighed by blessings. Some Christians, however, become depressed by the very nature of the Christian life and the things that they must face as a result of being Christians. These problem areas can broadly be divided into two categories: firstly, those areas affected by a distorted understanding of biblical teaching; and secondly, the things we face in the normal course of Christian life and service. Stress, physical disease or exceptional circumstances often reveal our weaknesses and cause us to re-evaluate our doctrines and our understanding of what God wants us to do with our lives. In this way, depression often serves a useful purpose. It forces us to face issues that we have previously been able to avoid and it challenges our attitudes and our actions. In the following two chapters we will address some of the important issues in these categories.

## The devil

Some depressed Christians wonder whether they are demon possessed. For many, it certainly feels like it! In seeking to understand the nature and source of depression, we would be foolish to leave out one of the key factors—Satan. As in our dealings with depression and sin, we must work from the general to the specific. In general, we are able to say that all sickness is a result of sin; in the same way we can say that Satan is behind all attacks of depression. This does not mean to say that every depressed person is in need of exorcism! Far from it. Untold damage has been done by those who take this view. We too must establish a balanced view on the subject lest we fall into the errors of either attributing everything directly to the devil; or rejecting any evidence of his activity. To understand the devil's role in depression we must first examine his person and work.

He is given many names and titles in Scripture; chiefly Satan (Matthew 4:10), and the devil (1 Peter 5:8). He is referred to as: the tempter (1

Thessalonians 3:5); the wicked one (Matthew 13:19); a murderer (John 8:44); a thief (John 10:10); a liar (John 8:44); the god of this age (2 Corinthians 4:4); a roaring lion (1 Peter 5:8); as one masquerading as an angel of light (2 Corinthians 11:14).

As the arch enemy of God he seeks to: lead people into sin (Genesis 3:1-6; Luke 22:31); blind the minds of unbelievers (2 Corinthians 4:4); inflict sickness (Acts 10:38); remove God's word from people's hearts (Matthew 13:19); sow tares among the wheat (Matthew 13:39); buffet God's servants (2 Corinthians 12:7); plant evil thoughts in the mind (John 13:2); and pervert the Scripture (Matthew 4:6). Whatever his intentions, he is limited in carrying them out. He cannot inflict sickness without God's permission (Job 1:10, 12); he cannot touch believers (Luke 22:31-32; 1 John 5:18) unless they make room for him in their lives (Ephesians 4:27; 1 Peter 5:7-9); and he must flee if resisted by the believer (James 4:7). Satan, however is a defeated enemy and subject to the eternal judgement of God. Christ came to defeat him (1 John 3:8); and on the cross, triumphed over him (Col 2:15). His destiny is settled (Matthew 25:41; Revelation 20:1-3).

Demons are the devil's ministers or angels. To deny the fact of demonic activity would be to fly in the face of biblical truth. Jesus drove demons from people (Matthew 8:16). He sometimes diagnosed physical symptoms of disease as being demonic in origin (Matthew 12:22-24; Mark 9:14-29). The Christian life is described in terms of spiritual warfare where we wrestle against, 'principalities, against powers, against the rulers of the darkness of this age, against spiritual *hosts* of wickedness in heavenly places' (Ephesians 6:10-20).

In the light of this, how are we to view the devil's work in depression? Firstly, we cannot rule out demonic activity. A depressed person could be under demonic attack. To deny this possibility would mean that we are only giving lip service to biblical truth. However, Jesus did not consider all sicknesses he encountered to be the result of demonic activity (John 9:1-7). He generally drew a distinction between demons and diseases (Luke 9:1; Mark 6:13).

Secondly, we are to recognize that Satan is a deceiver and will take every opportunity provided by our circumstances. He is far more likely to be successful by using our own weaknesses than by direct demonic attack which can be rebuked and forestalled by the believer. Paul had a 'thorn in the flesh'. He described it as, 'a messenger of Satan to buffet me'(2 Corinthians 12:7). Peter was personally responsible for his denial of Christ, but all the time Satan was sifting him as wheat (Luke 22:31-32). Our weaknesses are often the tools that the devil uses in trying to fulfil his purpose in bringing us down. As Thomas Brooks says, 'Whatever sin the heart of man is prone to, that the devil will help forward.'[1]

In the case of depression, the devil seeks to confuse us as to the origin of our condition. Depression can have a number of causes and combinations of causes. The devil may try to convince us that our particular depression is caused by personal sin and our failure to maintain an active spiritual life, whereas it may be primarily physical in origin. If he fails here, he may try a different tack by persuading us that our bodies are to blame and that there is no point in seeking spiritual and psychological solutions to our condition. Martyn Lloyd-Jones wisely warns us, 'We must not forget the existence of the devil, nor allow him to trap us into regarding as spiritual that which is fundamentally physical. But we must be careful on all sides in drawing the distinction because if you give way to your physical condition you become guilty in a spiritual sense. If you recognize, however, that the physical may be partly responsible for your spiritual condition and make allowances for that, you will be better able to deal with the spiritual.'[2]

How can we deal with this? I have already quoted Thomas Brooks. In *Precious remedies against Satan's devices*, Brooks deals with an area that is akin to depression in the Christian.[3] Satan's device is to suggest to a person that, 'surely his estate is not good, because he cannot joy and rejoice in Christ as once he could; because he hath lost that comfort and joy that once was in his spirit.' In other words, when we are depressed we are unable to enjoy even the spiritual riches we once had. This is due to our current mental state. Satan suggests that we have actually lost the source of our comfort and joy. Brooks' first remedy is to remind ourselves that, 'The loss of comfort is a separate adjunct from grace.' He goes on to say, 'There may be, and often is, true grace, yea, much grace, where there is not a drop of comfort, nor a dram of joy.' When Satan is deceiving us in this way we must remind ourselves, 'Though my comfort is gone, yet the God of my comfort abides; though my joy is lost, yet the seeds of grace remain.'

His second remedy is to consider, 'That the precious things that thou still enjoyest are far better than the joys and comforts thou hast lost'. We may lose the feelings that accompany our union with Christ, but we still have the fact of the union. Our 'sonship, saintship and heirship' remain. Brooks compares our comforts to a bag of silver, but our position in Christ to a box of precious jewels.

The third remedy is to look at the matter in eternal perspective. To consider, 'That thy condition is no other than what hath been the condition of those precious souls whose names were written upon the heart of Christ, and who are now at rest in the bosom of Christ.'

Fourthly, we must remind ourselves, 'That the causes of joy and comfort are not always the same.' Brooks speaks of our first source of joy and comfort, the witness of the Holy Spirit to our spirit of our changed nature. He goes on to say that the Spirit may, on occasions, grant us a special sense of God's presence; but this is not his usual office. Some of our joys and comforts spring from the newness and suddenness of the change in our condition. The experience may be dulled by time, but the fact remains.

Finally, 'God will restore and make up the comforts of his people. . . Though the candle be put out, yet God will light it again, and make it burn more brightly than ever.' God will not allow us to stay downcast for ever. The light will return to our lives and it will be brighter than before. We need to be patient, as Brooks says, 'Wait but a little, and thou shalt find the Lord comforting thee on every side.' This leads us into the subject of assurance.

## Assurance

Depression often challenges a Christian's standing before God. This can be a devastating experience for many, for whom losing the assurance of their salvation is the final straw. For some, the loss of a sense of assurance is the cause of the depression.

Assurance is both objective and subjective. It is based on the facts of salvation as revealed to us in the Bible. The Bible goes on to speak of the Holy Spirit bearing 'witness with our spirit that we are children of God (Romans 8:16; 1 John 3:24; 4:13; 5:10). This inner witness manifests itself in a sense of conviction that the believer is truly a child of God. The Scriptures instruct the believer to strive to have this assurance (Hebrews 6:11; 2 Peter

1:10). The apostle Paul was able to testify, 'For I know whom I have believed and am persuaded that He is able to keep what I have committed to Him until that Day.' (2 Timothy 1:12).

The subjective experience of assurance, however, differs in individual believers. The great Victorian bishop, J. C. Ryle, was sure that there were some truly regenerate believers who never experienced the full fruit of assurance. 'A child may be born with a great fortune and yet never be aware of his riches, may live childish, die childish, and never know the greatness of his possessions. And so also a man may be a babe in Christ's family, think as a babe, speak as a babe and, though saved, never enjoy a lively hope, or know the real privileges of his inheritance.'[4]

For most Christians the *feeling* of assurance fluctuates. 'None have assurance at all times. As in a walk that is shaded with trees and chequered with light and shadow, some tracks and paths in it are dark and others are sunshine. Such is usually the life of most assured Christians.'[5] This does not affect the *fact* of assurance. When we are depressed, we may not feel that we truly belong to the family of God. This feeling seems to be confirmed by the apparent absence of the marks of grace in our lives. We may not want to pray, or read the Bible. It is unlikely that we feel any desire to worship or have fellowship with other believers. We show little interest in the needs of others because we have become so preoccupied with our own condition. This confirms the feelings of self-doubt and self-loathing often experienced by the depressed. For some, this may be so intense, that they feel that their faith was merely an illusion. The true believer may well, at times, lack the sense of assurance that is rightfully his, but he does know where to go in order to retrieve it. In his lecture, *Spurgeon: His life and legacy*, Rev. Clive Anderson gives a wonderful illustration of this. Satan is attacking the very ground of Spurgeon's assurance. 'You are no saint', says the devil. 'Well if I am not, I am a sinner,' he replied, and Jesus Christ came into the world to save sinners, Sink or swim, I go to him; other hope have I none.'[6]

# Depression and the Christian life (2)

D
epression is often exacerbated when we look beyond the cause and try to discover the reason. The question, 'Why am I depressed?', is expanded to, 'If there is an all powerful, loving God, why am I depressed?' This is made more difficult for the Christian, because he calls that all powerful, loving God, 'Father'.

This question, as Gary Benfold outlines it, is real, relevant, and reasonable.[1] It is real because we cannot live on this earth without being aware of suffering. It is relevant because we will all inevitably become sufferers in one form or another. It is reasonable because it deals with crucial issues of man's relationship with God. The Christian will often ask the question when he endures physical or mental suffering as a *result* of his Christian life and service.

## Suffering

It is essential that the Christian has a biblical theology of suffering. The trouble is, we tend to avoid the question until it is brought home to us by personal suffering, and this is the wrong time for us to be addressing the whole question. We should address the issue before we enter the furnace. As Don Carson says, 'One of the major causes of devastating grief and confusion among Christians is that our expectations are false. We do not give the subject of evil and suffering the thought it deserves until we ourselves are confronted with tragedy. If by that point our beliefs—not well thought out and deeply ingrained—are largely out of step with the God who has disclosed himself in the Bible and supremely in Jesus, then the pain from the personal tragedy may be multiplied many times over as we begin to question the foundations of our faith.'[2]

The Bible teaches that God is omnipotent (Job 42:2; Matthew 19:26). His power is only limited by his nature and attributes; he cannot deny himself, sin or lie (2 Timothy 2:13; Numbers 23:19; Hebrews 6:18). God is love (1 John 4:16). In his providential care he works all things for the good of his people (Romans 8:28). In trying to understand the problem posed by the evil calamities that befall us, we must hold these truths in balance. To say that God bears no responsibility in these things denies his absolute sovereignty. Satan was only allowed to afflict Job with God's permission (Job 1:12). If I become depressed it is because God has allowed me to become depressed. If he has permitted depression to come upon me, it is done so in love. God did not stop loving Job.

How can we come to terms with this? The Bible gives no easy answer, but points to areas of truth that shed light on the dark areas in which we must walk. Firstly, God often allows man to reap the immediate consequences of his sin by withdrawing his restraining hand. Some human suffering is self inflicted through personal sin (Galatians 6:7-8). Secondly, God may allow suffering in order to recover and strengthen his people (Psalm 119:67; 1 Peter 1:3-9). Thirdly, suffering is part of a world under sin, but still under grace (John 16:33; Romans 5:20-21). God is still calling out his people from this world of sin and suffering until all the elect are gathered into his eternal kingdom (Mark 13:27; Matthew 24:31). Fourthly, we must not forget that our redemption came through suffering. God himself entered our human state to reconcile us to himself through his own suffering (Hebrews 5:5-9; 2 Corinthians 5:19). On the cross he experienced it (Hebrews 13:12); in the resurrection he triumphed over it (1 Peter 3:18-22); and in his return he will abolish it (1 Corinthians 15:22-28; 1 Thessalonians 4:16-18). As High Priest, he comforts his suffering people until the consummation of his kingdom (2 Corinthians 1:3-7).

Let us apply this to depression. If depression is primarily a disease, we must address the relationship between sickness and God's sovereignty. Any of the above reasons can apply to our condition. We may have brought depression upon ourselves by sinful behaviour or wrong thinking. Or, we may be enduring a time of trial in order to strengthen us. On the other hand, there may not be any apparent reason for our condition. The important thing is that, whatever the reason, God has not abandoned us. If we have sinned, he will forgive us (1 John 1:9); if we are being chastened, it is because he loves us (Hebrews 12:5-6); if we do not know the reason, surely he does (Isaiah 55:8-9).

Some have argued that it is never God's will that *any* should be sick, and that sickness of body or mind has no place in the victorious Christian life. Should we, therefore, simply pray for healing? Of course we should, Paul asked three times for his thorn in the flesh to be taken away (2 Corinthians 12:8)! Can God heal people today? Of course he can. To deny this would be to deny his sovereignty and omnipotence! But, to embrace a theology that does not allow for God's sovereignty in sickness is heading for disaster. What happens to the overwhelming majority who are not healed through prayer? Their faith is brought into question. It is sometimes suggested that there is some hidden blockage to healing that is yet to be discovered. The God who has 'promised' them healing through faith must be let off the hook and the onus is put on the sufferer. In my experience, many people cope with this by claiming a blessing through the healing prayer—a new calmness of spirit to enable them to cope with their sickness—a deep sense that the healing process has begun within them. This may well be the case for those who are suffering from an obviously physical condition whereby they are able to rationalize their position, but for someone suffering from depression the experience can be devastating. A depressed Christian needs to know that God has allowed this depression; that it is serving his eternal purpose; that healing will come in due time; and that, in the end, they will benefit from their suffering.

## Weary while doing good

'And let us not grow weary while doing good, for in due season we shall reap if we do not lose heart'(Galatians 6:9). Commenting on this verse of Scripture, Martin Luther writes, 'For it is an easy matter for a man to do good once or twice; but to continue, and not to be discouraged through the ingratitude and perversity of those to whom he hath done good, that is very hard.'3

The pressures of Christian life and service, along with all the other responsibilities we have, can lead to physical and mental exhaustion, causing us to become depressed. In one of his sermons, Spurgeon tells of such an instance in Luther's own life. Luther was going through a period of depression and despair. His friends, for fear of what he might say or do, decided that it would be best if the great reformer were to be alone. They persuaded him to have a period of solitude, to rest his brain and recover from the stress that was taking its toll on him. After a period of rest, Luther returned home, still in the same condition. Spurgeon goes on to say, 'I will now give you my own version of the method adopted for the great man's cure. He went home, but when he came to the door nobody welcomed him. He entered their best room, and there sat Catherine his wife, all dressed in black, weeping as from a death in the house. By her side lay a mourning cloak, such as ladies wear at funerals. "Ah," says he, "Kate, what matters now, is the child dead?" She shook her head and said the little ones were alive, but something much worse than that had happened. Luther cried, "Oh, what has befallen us? Tell me quick! I am sad enough as it is. Tell me quick!" "Good man," she said, "have you not heard? Is it possible that the terrible news has not reached you?" This made the Reformer the more inquisitive and ardent, and he pressed to be immediately told of the cause of sorrow. "Why," said Kate, "have you not been told that our heavenly Father is dead, and His cause in the world is therefore overturned?" Martin stood and looked at her, and at last burst into such a laugh that he could not possibly contain himself, but cried, "Kate, I read thy riddle,—what a fool I am! God is not dead, He ever lives, but I have acted as if He were. Thou hast taught me a good lesson."4

It may be argued that Luther, like Spurgeon himself, was temperamentally prone to such attacks. This may be the case, but there is a general cause that must be addressed. We are all human and can only take so much pressure. The classic biblical example of this is Elijah, whom James reminds us, 'was a man with a nature like ours'(James 5:17). On Mount Carmel we see Elijah bold and strong, standing against the forces of evil, gaining a glorious victory through faith in his God (1 Kings 18). At Horeb, we see a broken man, crying out to God, 'It is enough! Now, Lord, take my life, for I *am* no better than my fathers!'(1 Kings 19:4). Had Elijah simply lost his faith? Or, was there another reason for his condition? Could it not be that he was simply exhausted, and this had caused him to be filled with fear and self-pity?

This condition is sometimes referred to as 'burnout'. Anyone can be affected, but those who have responsibility for others are especially prone to it. The Christian ministry is a prime area where burnout can occur. This can also apply to those who have great responsibilities within a fellowship.

The minister is prone to burnout because of the nature of his calling. He is rarely able to measure the success or failure of his work. He is responsible for a group of people who are diverse in character and temperament, and he must try to keep his flock together. He must be sensitive to the needs of others, but not over sensitive when they do not respond. He is working with volunteers, who can withdraw their help at any time. He has no set working hours and often feels guilty when taking even legitimate breaks from the work. Above all, he is aware that he is God's servant and often feels that he has failed his master.

The worker in the fellowship has many of the same pressures, but must also fulfil his responsibilities at work and in the home. When the pressures increase in any of these areas, burnout can occur. For most Christians, church life is the oasis at which they refresh themselves in a weary week of work and responsibility. For others it can be the very opposite; where a tired, stressed person feels that the last ounce of moisture is being drained from them. It is essential for those involved in the Lord's work to recognize this and learn to deal with the matter before it reaches the onset of depression.

# Ourselves and others

Depression can stem from a false understanding of who we are and how we relate to others. Unless we develop a true picture of the self, as God intends us to be, we will always have problems in living and working in fellowship with others. This chapter deals with the problems we may encounter. Later chapters will point to their solution.

## The self

'Our greatest enemy is not the devil, but ourselves. What we need most of all is the conquest of self. To secure this, we need to know ourselves, and then be brought under submission to God and His Word and His will. Self-esteem is a great problem today, not because we have too little of it, but because we have too much of it.'[1] These words of Joel Beeke underline the need to develop a biblical understanding of the true nature and purpose of the self. Many of the problems associated with depression can be related to a distorted self-image. A depressed person generally becomes 'selfish'; full of self-loathing, even, in extreme cases, having suicidal thoughts; is unable to relate to other people's needs; and has a generally low self-esteem. One of the major goals in the healing process is to rebuild self-esteem. It is generally accepted that people with low self-esteem are prone to depression. Very few people, however, seem to question the nature and role of self esteem. It is almost universally accepted at face value as a 'must' for our children; the answer to many of the hurts inflicted upon us; and lack of it is often regarded as the cause of anti-social behaviour and crime. The subject will be dealt with in a later chapter, but for the moment we need to look at the nature of the self and see it in its biblical context. We do this because a distorted understanding of this important issue contributes greatly to many of the problems encountered by the Christian.

What is meant by 'the self'? To give a comprehensive list and evaluation of the major psychological theories in this area would take a whole book. They range from the physical to the metaphysical. I prefer to think of myself self as simply everything that goes to make up me, from my toenails to my eternal destiny!

Modern psychotherapeutic theories have majored on the self. The humanist has no God in whom he centres the meaning and purpose of his existence. As a result the centre becomes the self. This is considered to be the first step in a fulfilled and fruitful life. Paul Vitz goes as far as to argue that, 'psychology has become a religion, a form of secular humanism based on the worship of the self'.[2]

This problem has been compounded by Jung's archetypes of the collective unconscious. Like many philosophical and psychological theories, they have entered Christian thinking by the back door. Unnoticed and unheralded they have embedded themselves in the unwritten doctrines that have influenced the attitudes and practices of Christians that are often in conflict with the doctrines they espouse. Jung's theories are complex, and I would not want to do him an injustice by oversimplifying his views on the self and Christ, but there are certain principles we can state, principles that have affected the thinking of many. For Jung, the Christian idea of *salvation through Christ* represented the wholeness of self that the individuation process would ultimately achieve. In other words, salvation is a psychological process rather than a divine action. Symbols of the self and symbols of the God-image are the same thing. For Jung, the archetypal Christ was different from the Christ of biblical Christianity. The teaching of the Bible and the actions of Christian worship were steeped in psychological symbolism. A symbol, by its very nature, is subservient to the thing that it symbolizes. If Christ is a symbol of the self, then the self is superior to Christ. Christ, in effect, becomes our servant in the quest for self-fulfilment and self-satisfaction. How is this seen in Christian attitudes today? I believe that this can be seen quite clearly. The 'feel good' factor is paramount in much that passes as worship. Fewer people are prepared to commit themselves to a local fellowship in service. Biblical church discipline is rarely accepted. When the going gets tough even the tough get going—elsewhere!

Therefore, in addressing self-esteem we must ask, 'Whom do I esteem?' Is it a god who is image of my self; or a self who has been created in the image of God?

The Bible gives us the true picture of self-esteem. The Christian self is actuated in denial and death. In order to follow Christ we must deny ourselves (Matthew 16:24; Romans 8:17). The act of regeneration that is essential to Christian life is preceded by the death of the self (Romans 6:4). The Christian can only truly know his self when in living relationship with Christ. The apostle Paul puts it so wonderfully when he says, 'I have been crucified with Christ; it is no longer I who live, but Christ lives in me; and the *life* which I now live in the flesh I live by faith in the Son of God, who loved me and gave Himself for me.'(Galatians 2:20). Paul exhibits biblical self-esteem in the preface to his great discourse on the resurrection: 'But by the grace of God I am what I am, and His grace toward me was not in vain.'(1 Corinthians 15:10).

## Fellowship

'Alone I walk the peopled city, where each seems happy with his own. O friends I ask not for your pity—I walk alone.' During the nineteen-sixties I read a lot of poetry—most of which I have forgotten. These lines, however, have stuck in my mind. I think this is because they describe what it was like growing up in a city where liberated young people were encouraged to 'do their own thing'. The cult of individualism was in vogue—the times indeed, 'were a-changin.' My problem was that I didn't have a 'thing' to do; and even if I had, I did not have the wherewithal to do it! I suspect that most young people were in the same boat.

We did, however, swallow the philosophy of the day, and my generation and succeeding generations have perpetuated it. This has meant that we have difficulties in being part of a community; whether it be in the family, at school, at work, in social groups, or even in the church. When problems arise, or things happen that we do not like, our individualism is threatened and we tend to retreat from the problem. We are reluctant to accept responsibility and resent the discipline that is inevitable in being part of a group.

The Christian is not meant to be in isolation. He is redeemed (Galatians 3:13,14); adopted into the family of God (Ephesians 1:5); to become part of God's community, the church (Ephesians 5:22-32). His relationship to other believers is inseparable from his own, individual, relationship with God (1 John 4). As Mark Johnston puts it, 'There can be no place for individualism among God's people because we can never extricate ourselves from a responsible relationship with everyone else who has been united to Christ through faith. When it says, 'God sets the solitary in families' (Psalm

68:6), it is at least in part a pointer to local expressions of his wider family, where the needs of our spiritual loneliness can be met.'3

Being part of God's family brings great blessing and spiritual growth. It is an essential factor in our well-being. In the second part of this book we will be examining this in greater detail. Being part of a community, however, brings problems. The church that is meant to nurture us sometimes hurts us! To some degree, this is inevitable, as we are all fallible human beings. The Bible warns us of the damage that can be caused by the tongue (James 3). It is often the thoughtless or careless word that does so much damage.

Sometimes church life can cause us to be depressed. There are so many jobs to do and so few who are willing to do it. A person may be over-burdened by responsibilities. Instead of receiving offers of help and encouragement, he receives none; sometimes he is criticized for what he does. Others are willing, but do not have enough confidence to put them-selves forward. They are frequently overlooked when people are asked to take on new roles in church life. They may feel unwanted and unloved. Some people feel excluded from the friendships that develop within the local church. People tend to gravitate to those who are on the same wave-length, or the same social group; leaving some out on a limb, who are part of the 'fellowship' but who do not seem to be able to enjoy true fellowship.

We may become depressed as a result of false expectations. We can be disappointed by the failure of others to show the love we feel we deserve. We can compare ourselves with those who are 'successful' and feel inferior because we are not receiving the same blessings. Others often appear to be more spiritual than us, and by comparing ourselves with them we can sink into a state where we wonder whether we are even converted.

When a person is depressed, church life can often make matters worse. When we are depressed, we need to be treated sensitively, whatever the cause of our depression. In some cases, there may be cause for rebuke and correction, but this must be done in the right way and at the right time—and by the right person! On the whole, most Christians are helpful to those who are suffering depression, but there will always be those who think they know better, even though they know nothing of the circumstances of the depressed person. A depressed person may be told that his condition is a sin or the result of his own personal sin. He is wallowing in self-pity and only needs to 'look to Christ' for healing. Others may diagnose 'demon possession' and prescribe exorcism. On a number of occasions I have had depressed people come to me requesting exorcism, because they have been told that this is the cause of their condition. I am sure that a minority of church members view the pastor as a pharmacist rather than as a physician; there to dispense the 'medicine' they have prescribed.

Church life can cause or aggravate depression through no fault of its own. The fault sometimes lies with us. Proximity with other people can bring to the surface things that were hidden when we were able to retreat into our individualism. We may resent discipline, or be unable to accept genuine, constructive criticism. These things are an essential part of our maturity as Christians (2 Timothy 3:16; Romans 15:14). We may have problems relating to people; problems that we can no longer run away from now that we are part of the household of faith. These, and other difficulties may arise simply through the fact of fellowship. As a result, we may feel that fellowship is threatening rather than nurturing. This is something we must not run away from, and in the right kind of fellowship we will soon learn the joy of true Christian community.

# Positive aspects of depression

Samuel Rutherford said, 'When I am in the cellar of affliction, I look for the Lord's choicest wines.'[1] Is there any 'wine' for those who are afflicted with depression? Can there be anything positive in such an apparently negative experience? In this chapter we will seek to show that even in the midst of the darkest days of depression, something good is being done.

### Depression and the sovereignty of God

Depression often challenges our theology. One of the great doctrines that we are brought face to face with is the sovereignty of God. How we stand on this will affect the way in which we face our condition.

The Bible teaches the absolute sovereignty of God in all things (Isaiah 46:10;Ephesians 1:11). If a Christian is depressed, it is because the sovereign Lord has permitted it to be so. We have already seen this in the story of Job, 'I was at ease, but He has shattered me; He has also taken *me* by my neck, and shaken me to pieces; He has set me up for His target'(Job 16:12). The Psalmist, in praising God for his awesome works, clearly sees the sovereign hand of God in the afflictions suffered by his people, 'For You, O God, have tested us; You have refined us as silver is refined. You brought us into the net; You laid affliction on our backs.' (Psalm 66:10-11).

The Bible also teaches us that afflictions are permitted by God for our good. The words of the Psalm continue, 'We went through fire and through water; But you brought us out to rich *fulfillment*'(Psalm 66:12). It is important to realize that the afflictions we suffer in this life are not ultimately in the hand of fate or even the devil. The controlling power is in the hand of a God whom we call 'Father'. Depression, whatever its earthly cause, has a heavenly cause. It may not be easy for us to realize this when we are in the darkest depths of the condition, but the facts are presented clearly to us in the Word of God, 'Now no chastening seems to be joyful for the present, but painful; nevertheless, afterward it yields the peaceable fruit of righteousness to those who have been trained in it'(Hebrews 12:11). Depression is a blessing in disguise (2 Corinthians 4:17; Deuteronomy 8:5;

Job 5:17; 23:10; 1 Peter 1:7).

Therefore, it is essential that we are rooted and grounded in the doctrine of God's sovereignty so that depression will not take us by surprise and be so heavily disguised that we cannot recognize the presence of the one who loves us and has called us to be his children (1 Peter 4:12).

As we journey through life we encounter many mountains that block our path. There are a number of ways in which we reach the other side. Sometimes they can be removed simply by faith (Matthew 17:20). Sometimes the Lord will lead us around the mountain, through the valleys. We may encounter dark things within the valleys, but the mountain will always be in sight. Along the way he will lead us into rich pastures, and there he will feed us. On other occasions he will take us over the mountain. The climb will be tough and tiring, but the view will become more breathtaking as we reach the summit and begin our descent. There may, however, be a time when he chooses another way. He will take us by the hand and lead us into a dark tunnel. The experience will be disorientating, for we will have no point of reference to tell us where we are or where we are going. As we make our way through the darkness our only source of comfort is that he has us by the hand and he knows where we are going. We are, in effect, truly walking by faith and not by sight (2 Corinthians 5:7). Depression is very much like that tunnel. It places us solely in the hand of God, trusting that we *will* emerge into the light that awaits us on the other side.

## The purpose of depression

What useful purpose does depression serve? There are theories that link depression to the immune system and the need to conserve energy for the resistance of illness, but I will leave this to greater minds than mine! However, there are some things that clearly show us that depression can have a positive effect upon our lives and enable us to be better equipped to serve God. John Lockley puts this powerfully when he writes, 'Therefore if you are depressed, consider yourself privileged because God has some important work for you'.[2]

Depression reveals things and enables us to deal with issues that we may have previously ignored or even swept under the carpet. We are brought face to face with priorities.

During the rest of this chapter we will examine some of the positive aspects that may apply to our present condition. Before we do so, there is an important point to make. We must not fall into the trap of being too introspective. Even if we cannot find anything positive in our particular condition we must not despair. God knows us better than we know ourselves, and he sees the end from the beginning. There *is* a divine purpose in what we are suffering, and it *is* for our good and God's glory. Having said this, I do believe that most of us can relate to some, if not all, of the following suggestions.

## Depression and reformation

Most of us lead busy lives. Our time and energy are occupied with pressing issues of day to day life and activity. We have responsibilities to fulfill. Sometimes we wonder how we are going to achieve all that is expected of us in the time allotted to us. In order to cope with this we adopt habits of thinking and acting that become almost second nature to us. We have to do this to cope with the pressures of life. As a result of this, important matters are shelved so that we can deal with the present pressing claim upon our time. We have little or no time to contemplate the meaning and purpose of our lives and nurture our relationship with God. I am convinced that it is no coincidence that the alarming increase in cases of depression seems to correspond with the increasing secularization of the Lord's Day, even among Christians. This is why I deal with the subject in greater detail later in this book. Our maker has programmed into our timetable one day in seven on which we can rest and devote to eternal matters.

Depression slows us down and may even bring us to a complete standstill. We can no longer function as we did. At first we may have neither the inclination or the energy to do anything; but there will come a point where we must take stock of our lives. This is often at the point where we seek outside help.

When we start to examine our priorities we may be shocked to discover that we have given far too much attention to unimportant things, and far too little to the important.

We may discover that our depression is largely a result of wrong attitudes or ways of thinking. The Bible says, 'And do not be conformed to this world, but be transformed by the renewing of your mind, that you may prove what *is* that good and acceptable and perfect will of God.' (Romans 12:2). Depression may well enable us to do just that!

Depression may force us to make adjustments to our lifestyle. Our diet may have to change. We may have to take more exercise, learn to relax, and get more sleep. Most of us just muddle through from day to day unless we are forced to make such changes. Each case is unique, but as a rule, most of us will have to make some changes for the better.

It may be that some of us do not fit into the above category. Our lives are not filled with activity. One of the reasons we are depressed is because of that very fact. We have too little to do. We may feel worthless and unwanted by others. This too needs to be addressed. Why do we feel like this? What can we do to rectify it? The answers may be found in our attitude towards ourselves and those around us. There may be a deep seated cause for our condition that needs to be uncovered and dealt with. Depression forces us to address the issue and do something about it.

## Depression and humility

Depression is a humbling experience. On one hand it challenges our self-sufficiency, and on the other, it helps us to see our true value as children of God.

Spurgeon said, 'If the Christian did not sometimes suffer heaviness he would begin to grow too proud, and think too much of himself, and become too great in his own esteem. Those of us who are of elastic spirit, in good health, and are full of everything that can make life happy, are too apt to forget that all our own springs must be in him.'[3] It is easy, when everything seems to be going well, to consider ourselves to be self-sufficient. As a result of this, the onset of depression is masked or concealed. It is difficult, especially for the Christian, to admit that something is wrong, even to ourselves. Strange as it may seem, we can even become depressed without actually *feeling* depressed. We may be so skillful at coping with life, we are able to conceal the truth of our condition, even from ourselves. We may experience many of the symptoms of clinical depression yet still appear to be 'on top of things'. However, there has to be a point where we have to admit that there is something wrong and that we need help. For many of us this can be a humiliating experience. To admit that we cannot cope is a serious blow to our pride. This may be the only way that God can bring us to the point where we recognize our total dependence on him. To quote Spurgeon again, 'I owe more to the fire, hammer, and chisel than to anything else in my Lord's workshop.'[4]

In contrast to this, a person may be depressed because he feels that he has never been able to cope. We may have such a low opinion of ourselves and our ability to deal with life, we feel worthless. Low self-esteem has long been considered to be a major contributory factor in depression. We must not, however, confuse this with humility. Without minimizing or trivializing the deep rooted causes of such a position, we can say that in many cases it is a form of inverted pride. We have become so engrossed in our woeful state we are unable or unwilling to accept ourselves as God accepts us. This too needs to be dealt with, and depression forces us to face the issue squarely! True humility does not involve self-loathing and self-denigration; in fact it does not involve self at all.

## Depression and sensitivity

Some forms of depression can make us insensitive to the needs of others. This is especially true for those who are suffering from bipolar or manic depression. But, for most of us depression helps us to understand and sympathize with the frailty of others. Suffering induces sympathy with fellow sufferers. We can easily say to someone who is undergoing a form of trial or disease, 'I know how you feel'. However sincere our words, unless we have been in their place we do not really know how they feel! It is comforting to talk to someone who has been through what we are now going through. The classic example is our Lord himself, 'a Man of sorrows and acquainted with grief'(Isaiah 53:3). When we pray, we are not coming to one 'who cannot sympathize with our weaknesses, but was in all *points* tempted as we *are*, yet without sin.'(Hebrews 4:15).

The poet and hymn writer, William Cowper, suffered severe bouts of depression; yet out of this came some of the great hymns that have enriched the worship of the church for generations. Spurgeon spoke of his depression in his sermons. This struck chords in the hearts of many who heard him. Here was a man speaking, from the depths of his own experience, of a God who is able to meet our need.

Depression, rather than making us unfit for service, often makes us fit for service. For some of us it releases a sense of compassion and creativity that has been repressed. Sir Edward Elgar was once asked to give an opinion on a promising young musician. He is said to have commented, 'She will be great when something happens to break her heart'.

## Depression and sanctification

Here is a crucial issue for the Christian. Do we want to be happy more than we want to be holy? God is more concerned about our holiness than our happiness. Martyn Lloyd Jones has written, 'They alone are truly happy who are seeking to be righteous. Put happiness in the place of righteousness and you will never get it'[5]. If this is the case, depression may often play a role as the refining fire testing the genuineness of our faith (1 Peter 1:7). When in the grip of depression it is natural to assume that we are being hurt rather than being healed. Yet we must hold on to the truth that God is bringing us closer to himself and continuing the process of that will ultimately conform us to the image of his son. I often take comfort from George Swinnock's reference to Chrysostom's picture of the shepherd's dog taking the straying lamb into its mouth, not to bite it but to bring it safely home. Swinnock goes on to say, 'God's design in these sufferings is not to ruin, but to reform thee.'[6] When in the sharp teeth of depression, we are not being bitten but carried home.

## Preventative medicine for the soul

Considering this, what should our attitude be towards depression? If God is using it for his glory and for our ultimate well-being, should we resist it or simply embrace it as a gift? If we submit passively to it or do nothing to prevent it we are missing the point of its purpose. Depression is pain. Pain is God's gift to show us that something is wrong. In the physical realm, we seek to find the cause of the pain and deal with it. If the cause can be healed we take measures to ensure that it does not recur. If the cause has no cure we do all we can to alleviate the symptoms and reduce their intensity. Preventative medicine teaches us to do all we can to avoid getting the disease in the first place. So it is with our approach to depression.

Firstly, we must take measures to minimize the risk of becoming severely depressed. This is a kind of preventative medicine for the soul. Secondly, we must do all we can to be in as fit a state as possible so that if we do become depressed we are in the best possible condition to deal with it. The athlete is in a better state to deal with an injury than a sedentary person. Thirdly, if we do become severely depressed, we must do all we can to come through triumphant.

Is there anything we can do to prevent us slipping into a state of depression? Can we prevent the chain of moods and circumstances, that are part and parcel of everyday life, from becoming tightly knotted together? As we have seen in previous chapters, depression is a complex subject. Its causes and characteristics are many, and accurate diagnosis is difficult. However, we should not be daunted by this. The Bible tells us that we are 'fearfully and wonderfully made'(Psalm 139:14). The God who made us has the blueprint of our personalities and has given us so much sound advice in his Word.

Most of us are aware of the slogan, 'For the best results, follow the maker's instructions'. We have the common sense to take this advice before hastily using a new product, or carefully reading the instructions before assembling a new gadget or piece of furniture. Those of us who have failed to do this can testify to the disastrous results! We have become increasingly aware of the importance of preventative medicine. We make sure that our children are inoculated against diseases that have decimated infant populations in the past. We make sure that we have ample protection against disease when traveling to a distant land. We are aware of the dangers of the wrong kind of foods and the lack of exercise, and we act accordingly. There is no guarantee that we will not become ill; but preventative measures reduce the risk and, as a rule, enable us to make a quicker recovery.

The Bible contains some of the earliest accounts of preventative medicine. In the Old Testament we read detailed commandments by God in relation to his people's health and well-being: the Sabbath principle; forbidden foods; sanitation and personal hygiene; and the treatment of infectious diseases.

The Bible is also a book of preventative medicine for the soul. In the following chapters we will look at some of the important issues, before examining ways in which we can find help in coping with depression.

# Knowing yourself

Self knowledge is essential as a preventative and curative factor in depression. The Bible says, 'For if anyone thinks himself to be something when he is nothing, he deceives himself. But let each one examine his own work, and then he will have rejoicing in himself alone and not in another. For each one shall bear his own load.' (Galatians 6:3-5). Self knowledge helps us deal with the circumstances of life in an appropriate manner. In chapter four we looked at the way in which inappropriate reaction to events and circumstance contributed greatly to bouts of depression and even depressive illness. As we get to know ourselves we are able to respond to circumstances with a greater understanding of their true effect upon us. In other words, self-knowledge helps us to put things into perspective.

The Puritans were great advocates of self-knowledge. In many of their writings we see a deep understanding of the whole human condition. One of these great physicians of the soul was Richard Sibbes. In *The soul's conflict with itself*, he says that to remedy our casting down we must, 'cite the soul, and press it to give an account.'[1] This is exactly what David did in his question, 'Why are you cast down, O my soul?' (Psalm 42:5, 11; 43:5). Such questioning is the very opposite of what many of us do when we are depressed. Instead of speaking directly to our condition, we let our condition speak to us and become the governing factor of our feelings and actions. As Martyn Lloyd-Jones puts it, 'I suggest that the main trouble in this whole matter of spiritual depression in a sense is this, that we allow our self to talk to us instead of talking to our self.'[2] How can we effectively take control of our self unless we are acquainted with our self?

Richard Baxter was another great advocate of self-knowledge. He writes, 'He that is a stranger to himself, his sin, his misery, his necessity, etc., is a stranger to God, and to all that might denominate him wise and happy. To have taken the true measure of our capacities, abilities, infirmities and necessities, and thereupon to perceive what is really best for us and most agreeable to our case, is the first part of true practical saving knowledge.'[3] Baxter's wise words are applicable to every part of our being. We must take the 'true measure of our capacities and abilities'. We need to know what we are capable of receiving and doing. How many of us have become depressed because, primarily, we were unaware of this. Too many stressful things were happening at the same time; one more was added and it was the straw that broke the camel's back! We felt that we could cope with the extra workload, but we over stretched ourselves to the point where we were no longer able to function at all. We also need to know our 'infirmities and necessities'. We are created as unique individuals; our weaknesses and needs are different from others. We cannot all be strong in all areas; but if we feel that we are strong, or at least should be strong, where we are weak, we can end up in a state of despair. We all have needs. They are genuine, God given, needs and not simply products of the self. These needs should be met. How can we know what we need if we do not know our true self?

What Baxter is saying is biblical truth. It is not the product of modern selfist psychology. Of course, there is a great danger of taking this too far or approaching it in the wrong way. This has always been the problem with truth. It can be twisted, distorted, and counterfeited, until it becomes error.

Self knowledge must not be confused with the modern trend towards self-discovery. The Christian does not need to discover himself; God has already done that for him (Matthew 18:11; Luke 15:1-32; 19:10; John 18:9). We are saved to the uttermost (Hebrews 7:25). We are not delving into the hidden mysteries of our psyches, but simply uncovering the plain truth that God lays before us. The Bible gives us great encouragement in this, 'Eye has not seen, nor ear heard, Nor have entered into the heart of man The things which God has prepared for those who love Him' (1 Corinthians 2:9; Isaiah 64:4).

Baxter speaks of this as 'the first part of true practical saving knowledge'. We will look at these in greater detail.

Firstly, *true knowledge*. The Christian does not seek to know himself in order to become what he wants to be. True self-knowledge centres itself on a knowledge of the work of God within us. In it we see his hand as our creator and redeemer.

Secondly, *practical knowledge*. It is practical, because it deals with our daily experience and enables us to love and serve God as we ought. True self-knowledge is holistic in that it does not set one part of our being against another. For example, the Bible does not teach us to abuse, misuse, or neglect our bodies to elevate us to a plane of greater spiritual understanding; neither does it teach us to suspend the normal process of reasoning and common sense to know the mind of God. Of course, we must discipline our bodies in the right way; and we must exercise a faith that goes beyond our own finite understanding; but the more we get to know ourselves and the work of God within us, the more we will be able to see his hand in the daily outworkings of our lives.

Thirdly, *saving knowledge*. Self-knowledge examines the saving work of God within us. This is the most important issue that we face. It deals with assurance of salvation in Christ. It examines the sanctifying work of the Holy Spirit. It prioritises the things to which we should give the most attention. It echoes the words of our Lord himself, 'But seek first the kingdom of God and His righteousness, and all these things shall be added to you'(Matthew 6:33). We can slip into depression simply by failing to heed these words and allowing the anxiety produced by 'all these things' to consume us. An increasing awareness of God's saving work within us strengthens our faith in the promise that he is ordering all our circumstances for the good (Romans 8:28). This can be a valuable therapeutic experience. Forget what is happening, and see what God is doing. Then go back to what is happening. Do we not see it in a different light?

## The nature of self-knowledge

Knowledge is a powerful tool in our hands. Medical knowledge has stemmed the tide of disease and technical knowledge has transformed the lives of millions. Knowledge can vary in its depth. We can 'know' certain things merely as abstract information, or we can 'know' with a deep understanding and commitment to what we know. This is the kind of self-knowledge that God requires of us.

The first question we must ask is, 'What kind of self are we examining?' There are countless theories about the nature of the self. It is not within the scope of this book or substantially beneficial to our understanding of depression to deal with them. The problem the Christian has with his own understanding in this area is that he is a 'new creation' indwelt by the Holy Spirit; yet he is also one who still struggles with the old selfish nature! A balanced view is put by R. S. Anderson, when he writes, 'From this we can conclude that the self that God created within each person has been endowed with a capacity to love God as well as itself, and that sin does not utterly destroy the self. It is the failure of the self to overcome the destructive and disabling consequences of sin that renders it powerless unless renewed by God's grace. The 'new self' which is renewed through Jesus Christ in the power of the Holy Spirit is not a replacement for the self, but a renewing of the self that God gave to each person and that God loves in each person.'4

To truly know ourselves, we need to do more than examine our spiritual condition. We also need to know our physical and psychological capacities, strengths and weaknesses. After all, we are instructed in Scripture to present our bodies as living sacrifices and be transformed by the renewing of our minds (Romans 12:1-2).

## Knowing our bodies

As we have already seen, there are a number of physical factors associated with depression. If we are depressed, we cannot simply treat it as an aberration of the mind or behaviour. Physical disease and treatment, hormonal changes, and even our response to our environment can play their part. The more knowledgeable we are about our own physical condition, the more able we are to see these factors, and even if we are unable to deal with them directly, we can at least rid ourselves of the fear that we are going mad! Knowledge of our physiology also helps us develop a lifestyle that is less prone to deep depressive bouts.

We need to be aware of the uniqueness of our own particular physical and psychological make up. In advice given to preachers but, applicable to all of us, Martyn Lloyd-Jones stressed the importance of this: 'A man should get to know himself. I include in that that he should get to know himself physically as well as temperamentally and in all other respects. . . We also have different temperaments and natures, so you cannot lay down universal rules.'5 Our physical well-being and comfort are governed by these factors. Our capacities for hard work are limited by our state of health and age. Some of us require more sleep than others. Some of us feel more energetic and creative at different times of the day. As we shall see later in this chapter, we must not determine our life-style by comparing ourselves with others. After an evening meal that generally included champagne, cigars and brandy, Winston Churchill worked late into the night dictating his literary works to tired but dutiful secretaries. This was his most productive time. I assure you that this particular book could never have been written under that regime! Some of us are far more productive after a good night's sleep. Within the scope of our duties, we all need to develop routines that fit our physiology. What suits someone else does not necessarily suit you. Routines are not ruts, they are the lines on which we can move most smoothly and effortlessly through our day to day activities. Of course, in family situations compromises need to be made; but even the most harassed mother must be able to order her day to take into account her personal physical needs.

## Knowing our minds

We need to look at what is behind our thoughts, feelings and actions. Depression often forces us to do this. Many Christians seem to be locked into old ways of thinking about themselves and the world in which they live. By examining and challenging these things we are able to become liberated from their effect upon us. This is inevitably done when a depressed person seeks help from a psychotherapist. If we are prepared to examine ourselves before the onset of depression, we may not reach the point where we need professional help.

We need to know our own *temperament*. For example, there may be times or occasions when we know that we are going to overreact to what is happening. It is important that we become familiar with this and learn to deal with it in an appropriate way. As a preacher, I know that on a Sunday night I am going to feel depressed about the way in which I conducted the day's services and preached. Sometimes it reaches the point where I decide that it is time to give up preaching and leave it to those who do it well! I know preachers of a different temperament who cannot understand why I feel like this. Over the years I have examined the reasons why I have a tendency to feel this way. One reason is that I feel a great sense of responsibility to God and to my congregation, and that only my best will do. I rarely feel that I have given my best. On a less noble note, I recognize that there is a strong self-centred element in this. If I have 'performed' badly, what will the congregation think of *me*? Any adverse comment made to me, immediately after I have preached, wounds my pride and can easily plunge me into a bout of self-pity. Also, I find preaching mentally draining. On Sunday nights I am exhausted! Self-knowledge helps me deal with this. I know that much of my suffering is due to my temperament, and if I let him, Satan will use this to make me give up the very thing that God has called me to do. On Monday morning, I know that my mind will not be able to cope with heavy intellectual work, so I busy myself with less demanding things. I also know that by Monday afternoon I will be able to look back on the previous day in a calm and reasonable way. It is not long before I am longing to get back in the pulpit again. We must get to know our individual temperaments and learn to think and act accordingly.

We must also get to know our *weaknesses and limitations*. We can easily become depressed when we have 'failed' in areas where we were never really capable of 'succeeding'. While we are aware that God can call the most unlikely people to do great things for him, we must also recognize that, as a rule, the Lord, who knows our capabilities, will not call us to do that which is beyond us. It is not beyond reason to assume that God knew the diplomatic skills of Esther and Daniel, and the intellectual capabilities of Paul, before he called them to their appointed tasks. Only God knows our true capabilities; but it is also important that we have some understanding of them too. This is not just applicable to Christian service but to life itself. Some people are depressed because they are in a job that they can only just cope with. Sadly, the pressures of the commercial world have increased the trend towards this. For some there seems to be no way out, but for many, it would be better to step one rung down the ladder into any area within their capabilities, for the sake of their own well-being. I am aware that this is easier said than done; but some people are pushing themselves to, and beyond, the limit of their capabilities to support their current life-style. Surely it is better to change our life-style than to have it dramatically changed for us by mental or physical breakdown!

We must also recognize our weaknesses and limitations in the home and family. We will never be perfect husbands, wives, parents, grandparents, or children. We need to learn to accept that we are loved for who we are and not for what we do.

None of this presupposes that we are simply to accept ourselves uncritically. Weaknesses can be turned into strengths; and the boundaries of our capabilities can be stretched. Self-knowledge enables us to do this in the right way, encouraging us to move forward without stretching ourselves to breaking point.

We need to know our *temptations*, for we can be sure that Satan knows them, and is behind them (2 Corinthians 2:11; 11:3). The Bible teaches us that we will all endure temptation, but God will enable us to stand firm in the midst of it (1 Corinthians 10:13). If we know the areas in which we will endure the greatest temptation, we are more able to resist and win the day. As Richard Baxter says, 'It is a self-ignorance that makes men rush upon temptations, and choose them, when they customarily pray against them. Did you know what tinder or gunpowder lodgeth in your natures, you would guard your eyes and ears, and appetites, and be afraid of the least spark.'[6] If we are aware of our temptations and their explosive power in our lives, we are better equipped to avoid situations in which we are tempted, or, at least dampen the gunpowder so that it will not readily ignite!

I remember hearing the story of a young man who asked his pastor to pray for him. On his way to and from work, the man passed a particular book shop. In the shop window were books that filled his mind with sinful thoughts. Whenever he passed by, he was drawn to look into the window. He asked that the pastor might pray that he would be given power to enable him to look the other way. The wise pastor did pray with him, but he also drew him a sketch map that would enable him to walk to work without having to pass the book shop at all. We may have temptations that are far different from this particular young man, but the principle still applies. It is better to give Satan as little material to work with as possible. Self-knowledge enables us to do this.

Chapter 15

# Being yourself

How are we to know ourselves? The Bible gives us invaluable advice in this area. Let us go back to the passage that we quoted at the beginning of chapter fourteen, 'For if anyone thinks himself to be something when he is nothing, he deceives himself. But let each one examine his own work, and then he will have rejoicing in himself alone and not in another. For each one shall bear his own load.'(Galatians 6:3-5). We learn a number of things from these words. Firstly, we must be aware of the danger of self-deception (Jeremiah 17:9). We must examine our hearts in an open and honest way. This will not be easy as we may have a tendency to think too highly of ourselves, or, if we are depressed, to think too lowly of ourselves. The word 'examine', in the context of this passage, means, 'put to the test'. Jeremiah urges us to, 'search out and examine our ways' (Lamentations 3:40). This indicates that we must do this with great diligence, for such self-examination goes against our fallen nature (James 1:23-24). Some people are perfectly happy to live in the dim light of half-truth about themselves. It is only when trial or tribulation comes that they realize the folly of this position. If we know our hearts and our standing before God, our assurance of salvation is clearer to us when the dark days come.

Depression, whatever its cause, can cast a shadow over the brightest faith. Derek Prime related the story Spurgeon used to tell, of a poor bedridden woman whose faith once bright, had gone under a cloud and suffered total eclipse. One day when he was visiting her, she said to him, 'I don't think that I have any real faith nowadays or any true love to Christ whatever.' But Spurgeon was a wise man. He did not argue with her. He took a piece of paper, and walked to the window and wrote the words, 'I do not love the Lord Jesus Christ.' Then he brought it back, with a pencil and said, 'Now, just sign that.' She took it and read it, 'I can't sign that,' she cried. 'It's not true. I'd be torn to pieces before I'd sign that.' 'But you said it just now,' he answered, 'you know what you said.' 'Ah, but I could not put my hand to it,' she answered. 'Well then,' Spurgeon went on, 'I suspect you do love him after all.' 'Yes, yes,' she cried, 'I see it now! I do love him—Christ knows that I love him!'[1]

Secondly, we are to examine ourselves in the right way. Paul makes it quite clear that we are not to do this by comparing ourselves with others, 'But let each one examine his own work, and then he will have rejoicing in himself alone, and not in another'. True self-knowledge cannot be obtained by looking at ourselves in the mirror of someone else's life and actions. There are two great dangers in doing this. We can compare ourselves favourably with others by concentrating on their negative characteristics. The Lord Jesus ridiculed this attitude in his words, 'Hypocrite! First remove the plank from your own eye, and then you will see clearly to remove the speck from your brother's eye.'(Matthew 7:5). It is easy for our fallen natures to deceive us into thinking that such an approach constitutes self-examination. On the other hand, we can do the very opposite. Other people can appear to be more spiritual and capable in comparison with ourselves. This makes us feel inferior. In doing so we never get to see the wonderful work of grace that is taking place in our own lives. This is both dishonouring to God, who is at work within us; and instrumental in making us vulnerable to depression. If we are to examine ourselves in a mirror, let that mirror be the Word of God.

It is no coincidence that a God-given place of self-examination is the Lord's Table. The focus of attention is the Lord himself. Our minds are occupied with thoughts of his atoning death, his heavenly intercession and his glorious appearing. This is preceded by self-examination (1 Corinthians 11:28). In doing so we are to look at our relationship with others; not to compare ourselves with them, but to do the very opposite. We do not look at them to see reflections of ourselves, but to see the Lord's imprint upon them. We examine ourselves that we may see the wrongs that need to be put right in our relationship with them, for to love them is to love Christ (1 John 4:20-21).

What are we to look for in this kind of spiritual self-examination? Paul, again, helps us here. 'Examine yourselves as to whether you are in the faith. Test yourselves. Do you not know yourselves, that Jesus Christ is in you?— unless indeed you are disqualified'(2 Corinthians 13:5). This is the most important area of self-examination. Our whole eternal destiny hinges on this. We can easily become depressed because we have failed to do this on a regular basis. We have assumed, all along, that we are Christians yet, because we have not tried and tested our faith ourselves, when a great trial appears, our salvation is brought into question. By examining and testing ourselves in this way, we establish objective truths about our standing with God. The problem we face when we are depressed is that we tend to become almost totally subjective. The focus of attention becomes *our* faith. What Paul urges us to do is to see whether we are in *the* faith. He goes on to say, 'Do you not know yourselves, that Jesus Christ is in you?' Self-knowledge acts like a compass, enabling us to check our position and change direction if we are off course (Lamentations 3:40).

We must not be afraid of self-knowledge. As we have seen, it is essential for our health and well-being. It is commanded by God that we may make our 'call and election sure'(2 Peter 1:10). It enables us to be what God intends us to be.

## Being yourself

I wonder how many of us would rather be someone else? I am sure that some people could add that they would rather be somewhere else too! On the other hand, I have often met people whose main complaint in life is that they cannot be themselves; they feel that in every relationship and situation, they are playing some kind of role that will make them acceptable to others. From time to time we can all relate to both positions.

Most of us have momentary bouts of envy when we encounter someone who has the qualities we desire for ourselves. We all have to play roles of one kind or another in order to function in a complicated social environment. Problems occur when we reach the point where either position becomes so dominant we either do not want to be ourselves, or we feel that we cannot be ourselves. Both situations can easily lead to depression.

For the Christian, the problem is compounded by the fear of becoming 'self' centred. Popular psychology books speak of self-actualization and self-realization, while the Bible speaks of self-denial. We may reason that the right approach is not to think of self at all. In a sense, this is right. We would be happier, and the world would be a better place, if we thought less of ourselves and more of others. But, because we live in a sinful world, the question of being ourselves has to be addressed. We do not live in a neutral environment. As we have already seen, our lives are shaped by many factors and influences. By becoming our true selves, as God would have us be, we nullify the effect of the world, the flesh and the devil. To present ourselves to God as living sacrifices for his service, we have to take our selves out of the hands of others. To do this, we must beware of the trap of selfism, but, at the same time, recognize that we have a duty to God to be what he intends us to be.

## False evaluation

False evaluation of the self occurs in two ways. The first, and most obvious, is to think too highly of ourselves. One of the reasons for true biblical self-knowledge is that we are so easily deceived in this matter. (Galatians 6:3). Lack of self-esteem is considered to be one of the most common psychological factors in depression. We need to be aware, however, that the Bible gives us due warning of esteeming ourselves too highly (Psalm 36:2; Matthew 23:12). The plain fact is, because of sin, we are unable to make an accurate evaluation of ourselves (1 Corinthians 8:2; Proverbs 3:7).

The second cause for false evaluation is the evaluation placed upon us by others. This is a double edged sword. If others value us highly, there is a danger that we can develop a false image of our importance. The Bible warns us about this in the matter of selecting leaders in the church (1 Timothy 3:6). We see this danger in the world of the 'celebrity', who starts to believe his own publicity, and considers himself to be above the norms of social behaviour, even the law! More relevant to depression, however, is the person whose life has been shaped by negative evaluation. Many people have false evaluations of themselves because throughout their lives they have been 'put down' by others. As children we tend to believe everything people say about us. We are unable to separate the truth from the fiction. Our confidence can become so shattered, we spend the rest of our lives looking for other people's approval. In effect, we spend our time asking others to tell us who we really are! We have seen in the previous chapter that true self-knowledge does not come through comparing ourselves with others; neither does it come by over valuing their opinions.

For example, none of us enjoy being criticized. We are aware, however, that we are not above criticism. The person criticising may be genuinely pointing out a fault so that we can correct it. On the other hand, he may be the type of person who criticizes others to enhance his own self-esteem. Whatever the motive, our value is not affected by the criticism. Problems occur when we cannot separate criticism of what we *do* with criticism of who we *are*. This may be caused by childhood experiences. Many of us have trouble with relationships because of this. We fail to realize that some of our fiercest critics are our best friends. As a result we spend our lives seeking the approval of others, and fail to take opportunities for fear of further criticism. Some people are almost incapacitated because of this.

This can be illustrated by the way in which we use the words, 'yes' and 'no'. Jesus said, 'Let your 'Yes' be 'Yes', and your 'No,' 'No'. For whatever is more than these is from the evil one.' (Matthew 5:37). At the risk of taking a text out of context, we can say that here is a great psychological truth as well as a theological one. How we use these words can be a diagnostic tool in evaluating ourselves. How often do we use the word, 'yes', when we really want to say, 'no'? At the risk of upsetting others and making them think less of us, we are often persuaded to do things we do not want to do. We all do this to some extent, but the danger occurs when we feel unable to say 'no' to anything. People can be easily led into sin, unhappy relationships and even the wrong careers because of this! On the other hand, how often do we say 'no' when we want to say 'yes'. Opportunities present themselves, we feel that we can take them, and then doubts creep in. We can almost hear a voice saying, 'You will not be able to do that'. How many opportunities have passed us by because of this? We all have healthy feelings of self-doubt, but we must not, however, be crippled by doubts that have their origin in false evaluation. The devil will often use these to try to thwart the purposes of God in our lives.

## True evaluation

How are we to know our true worth? The only one who can place a true evaluation upon us is God. His judgement is not impaired by sin; neither does he have any need to demean us to enhance his own glory. What are the criteria for the evaluation of a Christian? We can illustrate this from the art world. When a painting is for sale, a number of factors determine its value: the identity of the artist, the condition of the painting, and the price someone is willing to pay for it. The painting itself, as a piece of canvas covered in pigment, is of little worth. If we look at God's evaluation of the Christian, what do we find? Firstly, he is revealed as the artist. He created us (Genesis 1:26), and he is the master craftsman of our salvation, from beginning to end (Ephesians 1:4-5; Romans 8:29-30). Secondly, he is our preserver (Philippians 1:6; Jude 1:24). Thirdly, he was prepared to pay a great price for us (1 Peter 1:18-19). Whatever we may think of ourselves, and whatever false evaluation others may place upon us, the only true evaluation is God's.

If you are a Christian, pause for a moment and consider the following Scriptures. You are accepted in the beloved (Ephesians 1:6); a joint heir with Christ (Romans 8:17); the salt of the earth, and the light of the world (Matthew 5:13-14). What does this do for your self-esteem? Surely it removes the 'self' element completely, as your true value is found in what God has done for us in his Son. The apostle Paul describes the perfectly integrated Christian in the following way, 'I have been crucified with Christ; it is no longer I who live, but Christ lives in me; and the *life* which I now live in the flesh I live by faith in the Son of God, who loved me and gave Himself for me.'(Galatians 2:20).

# Self-acceptance and self-denial

## Accepting ourselves

If we evaluate ourselves in a biblical way, we must go on to accept ourselves as God accepts us. This helps us deal with guilt feelings and feelings of self-worthlessness. Many of us find self-acceptance difficult. We conscientiously try to be consistent in our obedience to the command to forgive others (Matthew 6:14-15); we are fully aware that forgiveness is essential to our happiness (Matthew 5:7); yet, we can be merciless in our dealings with ourselves. We can forgive another person time after time (Matthew 18:21-22), yet harbour a grudge against ourselves for one fleeting error. Are we aware that such a position is an affront to God? If we pray, 'And forgive us our debts, As we forgive our debtors'(Matthew 6:12), and do not forgive ourselves, we are asking God to do something that we are not prepared to do. We are setting ourselves above God. Self-acceptance is true humility; self-rejection is the very opposite.

People often reveal their lack of self-acceptance by concentrating on what they consider to be their negative features. The boom in cosmetic surgery; and the alarming numbers of cases of anorexia and bulimia are dramatic examples of this. People are easily fooled into trying to conform to an ideal laid down by others. Even more alarming, are the cases of 'copy cat' suicides committed by young people after the death of a revered pop idol. On a less dramatic note, most of us are a little embarrassed when someone tries to pay us a compliment. All these things add up to reveal that in the midst of a selfist society, there is still an alarming lack of understanding as to the nature of true self-acceptance.

What is self-acceptance? I use the term 'self-acceptance' in preference to 'self-esteem'. In doing so, I recognize that many Christians will be comfortable using 'self-esteem' to describe the very things I am dealing with in this section. I am also aware that, many Christian psychologists use the term technically, and take great pains to distance themselves from its humanistic connotations. Whatever term we choose to use, the important issue is that we recognize the centrality of Christ and not the self!

Self-acceptance is a psychological fruit of the gospel. In 1 Corinthians 15, the apostle Paul deals with the great subject of the resurrection. Before he begins his argument, he re-introduces the gospel to his readers. In doing so he reminds us that the gospel affects every area of our lives, in this world and in the world to come.

Firstly, he presents evidence for the gospel—it is a gospel for the *mind* (1 Corinthians 15:3-7). He speaks of the death, burial and resurrection of Christ as being, 'according to the Scriptures'. He goes on to introduce an impressive series of witnesses to the event.

Secondly, he speaks from his own experience—it is a gospel for the *heart* (1 Corinthians 15:8). He believes the gospel, not on the evidence alone, but because he has met the risen Christ. In describing his experience, he says, 'Then last of all he was seen by me also, as by one born out of due time'. He did not see Christ in the flesh. His encounter with the Lord was in a blinding light and a voice from heaven. In human terms, he was not ready to meet with the Lord; it was sudden and unexpected. He was like a premature baby thrust from the womb into the world. Conversion is like that. It takes place under God's control and God's timing.

Thirdly, he speaks of the effect of the gospel—it is a gospel for the *life* (1 Corinthians 15:9-10). When Christ takes hold of us and places us in the kingdom of God, we become what God wants us to be, and ultimately find ourselves. The immediate effect is one of total humility. This has nothing to do with our virtues or efforts; it is all down to God's grace. Paul sees this clearly when he says, 'For I am the least of the apostles, who am not worthy to be called an apostle, because I persecuted the church of God'. In another letter, he lists many things that could easily be used to enhance his self-esteem, but he counts them worthless in the light of what Christ has done for him (Philippians 3:4-11). True humility focuses the attention away from the self and places it on Christ. George Whitefield, when seeing the bodies of criminals hanging from the gallows at Tyburn, uttered the immortal words, 'There, but for the grace of God, go I.' True humility, in the light of the gospel, leads on to true self-acceptance. Paul can now go on to see his life and service for his Lord in perspective. He says, 'But I laboured more abundantly than they all'. As a result of the gospel, he has dedicated his life to its promulgation. He is not boasting of his success, but neither is he making light of his efforts. He can now rejoice in what God is doing in him and through him. This is made clear by the words, 'Yet not I, but the grace of God *which* was with me'. Such was Paul's focus upon the grace of God at work within him, he could say with true humility, 'The things which you learned and received and heard and saw in me, these do, and the God of peace will be with you'(Philippians 4:9). How many of us could speak like that?

The key to self-acceptance is found in Paul's words, 'But by the grace of God I am what I am, and His grace toward me was not in vain'(1 Corinthians 15:10). There is no complacency here. Paul knows that he is not perfect. He still struggles with the old man within, but he recognizes that God is at work in his life. Here is the balanced view we need to take of our own lives. The craftsman is at work; the masterpiece is taking shape; the rough edges are being removed; and although we cannot see the finished article, we trust the wisdom and skill of the craftsman. John Newton was fully aware of this, when he said, 'I am not what I ought to be! Ah! how imperfect and deficient! I am not what I wish to be! I abhor that which is evil and would cleave to that which is good! I am not what I hope to be! Soon, soon, I shall put off mortality, and with mortality all sin and imperfection! Yet, though I am not what I ought to be, nor what I wish to be, nor what I hope to be, I can truly say that I am not what I once was, a slave to sin and Satan; and I can heartily join with the apostle, and acknowledge, "By the grace of God I am what I am!"'.

By accepting ourselves, we are accepting what God is doing. We may not have any worth of our own, but we are trophies of grace. When a trophy is paraded before others, the attention is not on the trophy itself but on the one who holds it high. Jay Adams says, 'There is great potential in the new life that we have in Christ, but we will never begin to realize it if we sit around thinking about how worthy we are'.[1]

## Denying ourselves

Self-acceptance and self-denial are complementary factors in a right attitude towards the self. Self-acceptance recognizes and rejoices in what God is doing in our lives; self-denial is the means by which we prevent the old nature from keeping us from the blessings that accrue to us from being in Christ. As Edward Griffin says, 'Self-denial lies at the foundation of all practical religion, as supreme love to God lies at the foundation of all the religion of the heart'[2]. Self-denial is a necessary part of a person's walk with Christ, from beginning to end (Matthew 16:24; Luke 14:26-27; 2 Corinthians 5:13-15). It is the denial of the supremacy of the self over Christ. Walter Chantry gives a good overview, when he writes, 'Self-denial is a practice which lies very near to the heart of true religion. Without its exercise there can be no conversion to Christ. Qualities most basic to a Christian frame of heart—notably humility and meekness—would dissolve without its active expression. Self-denial awaits the sons of God as they enter upon their private devotions. It stands at the threshold of witnessing and other service to our holy Lord. It is a painful element in each struggle after holiness. Denial of self is the key to the solution of numerous practical questions that perplex the sober-minded believer of today. A right understanding of this basic biblical demand would silence a host of errors regarding evangelism, sanctification, and practical living'[3]. Self-denial always focuses our attention on Christ and not on our selves.

It is important to fully understand the nature and place of self-denial in the life of the Christian. Self-denial is not in direct competition with our own happiness. There may be times when to deny ourselves for the sake of God, or for the common good, will mean that we will endure periods of unhappiness. We must, however, beware of the foolish notion that by constantly denying ourselves God given happiness and pleasure we are practising true self-denial. This was the grave error made by so many of the ascetics who thought that by acts of self-punishment and sacrifice they were obeying Christ's call to take up their cross and follow him. Their focus of attention was mistakenly directed to the self rather than to the grace of God at work within them. How many Christians still choose to wear the hair shirt rather than the garment of praise! We can easily be reduced to the ludicrous situation of believing that, 'If we enjoy it, it cannot be God's will!' I remember going through this phase myself, and I can still detect remnants of the condition within me. I still get occasional flashes of guilt when I sit in my study, doing what I enjoy best, reading and writing, while members of my congregation are out at work earning money to pay my stipend. I can only overcome this by marvelling at the grace of God, that he should call me to do what I enjoy the most!

Parents practise self-denial for the sake of their children's welfare and happiness. Is it wrong to be happy because they are happy? On the other hand, there will come a time when we must deny ourselves the joy of their presence in the home and let them go for the sake of their future happiness. The important element in this is that satisfaction is not found in our sacrifice but in the results that accrue from it.

Self-denial takes a number of forms. Firstly, it is the denial of the power of sin in our lives. This is to be a constant practice. The apostle Paul urges his readers to, 'Put to death your members which are on the earth: fornication, uncleanness, passion, evil desire, and covetousness, which is idolatry'(Colossians 3:5; see also Romans 8:13; Galatians 5:16). Peter echoes Paul's words, 'Beloved, I beg you as sojourners and pilgrims, abstain from fleshly lusts which war against the soul.'(1 Peter 2:11).

Secondly, we are to deny ourselves for the common good. This was evident in the New Testament church, where people were drawn from different cultural backgrounds. Paul deals with this in Romans 14, where he expounds the law of liberty and the law of love. He urges the strong to deny themselves legitimate things for the sake of the weak, 'We who are strong ought to bear with the scruples of the weak, and not to please ourselves'(Romans 15:1). Many have denied themselves to the point where they have willingly laid down their lives for others. Paul was even willing to deny himself the joy of immediate heavenly glory for the sake of God's people (Philippians 1:23-24).

Thirdly, self-denial always places the will of God above our own interests. As Griffin says, 'Nothing is self-denial but the subjection of our natural feelings generally to the will of God and all our interests to his interest'[4]. There may be times when this will cause us great pain; but, in the end, it will abound to our joy (Luke 18:29-30).

It may seem that we have strayed from the subject of depression. But this is not the case. Lack of self-denial will eventually lead to some kind of depressive experience. The gravitational pull of self-gratification will always lead us downward. This is illustrated in the story of the prodigal son, who gratified every desire of the flesh and reaped the results (Luke

15:11-32). When we are steered by the rudder of self-interest, we turn on the one who has led us on to the rocks. In the end we begin to loathe ourselves for allowing ourselves to be in this position. The Christian who allows selfish desires and pursuits, however seemingly legitimate, to encroach upon his walk with God will, in the end, blame himself. How wonderful it is to know that, if we return to God in repentance and faith, we have a loving heavenly Father who will forgive us and restore us.

The wrong kind of self-denial will also make us prone to depression. It is impossible for any of us to deny ourselves in order to atone for our sin. Even if we were to lay down our lives, the sacrifice would not be acceptable to God. If you are denying yourself happiness in the mistaken idea that you are in some way making up for past sins or mistakes, think again! Nowhere does the Bible instruct you to do this. In fact, it commands you not to do it, 'For You do not desire sacrifice, or else I would give it; You do not delight in burnt offering. The sacrifices of God *are* a broken spirit, A broken and contrite heart—These, O God, You will not despise'(Psalm 51:16-17). Stop punishing yourself as an offering to God, and bring your broken spirit and contrite heart to him—he has made the atoning sacrifice.

## Self-control

The Bible says, 'And do not be conformed to this world, but be transformed by the renewing of your mind, that you may prove what *is* that good and acceptable and perfect will of God'. (Romans 12:2). Self-control is an important factor in being ourselves. We have inherited old patterns of thinking that may have to be changed. Many people think of self-control only in terms of pleasure denied. There is a lot more to it than this. We have already noted that we do not live in a neutral environment. We are all controlled by someone. The question is, 'By whom?' Some may feel that their lives are controlled by others. Demands placed upon them leave them no time to be themselves. Others may be controlled by past experiences. Patterns have been laid down for their lives and they dutifully conform to them. Others may claim to be in control because they are governed by their feelings. They only do what they feel like doing. As we have seen, feelings can be the biggest tyrants in our lives. Let me remind you of some wise words we quoted in the previous chapter, 'The main trouble in this whole area of depression in a sense is this, that we allow our self to talk to us instead of talking to our self.'5 When we are depressed, we are controlled primarily by our feelings. We are fully aware that this should not be so, but we feel that there is little we can do about it. It is as if the sovereignty of God extends everywhere except to how we feel! The only way in which we can experience the lordship of Christ in this area is through self-control. This is God's chosen way of exercising control over us. Self-control is listed among the fruit of the Spirit (Galatians 5:22-23), yet it is not something we passively receive from God, it has to be worked at (2 Peter 1:6-7). Self-control is not the self controlling us, but God the Holy Spirit exercising control over the self. The new nature is controlling the old nature. By exercising self-control we are able to know the will of God, and enabled to obey it (Romans 12:2). It was an integral part of the gospel message that Paul preached to Felix and Drusilla (Acts 24:25).

Many people undergoing counselling for depression need to be taught assertiveness. In general terms, assertiveness is being able to say what you mean and mean what you say. We have already looked at the way we use the terms, 'yes' and 'no'. By practising self-control we are being assertive. We are no longer slaves to our own sinful natures; neither are we puppets operated by others, either from the past or present. Although we value the opinion of others and respect their rights and needs, we are not governed by them; we are not afraid to disagree with them; nor are we afraid to stand up for that which we believe to be right.

Lack of self-control can cause a number of problems. For example, we may agree to a certain course of action that we are not happy about. Rather than voice our doubts at the outset we go along with the situation for fear of upsetting those involved. As things progress we become increasingly uneasy, but it also becomes increasingly difficult for us to say how we truly feel. As the course of action reaches its fulfilment, one of two things can happen. We can either reach the point where we can no longer contain ourselves, or we can continue to go along with the situation. If we do the former, we may feel guilty because we have misled others. If we choose the latter we will feel angry with ourselves, and may even resent those involved. Both are potent factors in depression. If we are assertive, that is, able to exercise self-control, we will avoid situations like this.

How do these things relate to being ourselves; and how can it help us deal with depression? We must not be afraid to know ourselves. Every part of us is the unique creation of God. Although we all want to feel wanted and valued by others, we must not accept any valuation of our worth other than from God. Having given ourselves over to the evaluation of God, we must accept it heartily. We must learn to deny ourselves in a balanced and godly way. We must engage in the spiritual, psychological and physical exercise of self-control, knowing that joy awaits us when we do this. These things should be part of our daily lives, and equip us to cope with the depressive experiences of life. For some, depression itself brings them to the point where they must face these things. If so, then however unpleasant the experience, there is a positive outcome.

# Perspective

Witnesses to an event give varying accounts of what they see and hear. Viewed from different angles and distances, even an inanimate object can be described in different ways. Increase the complexity with a moving event and the descriptions will vary immensely. Include other factors, such as, attention, memory, prejudice, emotion, and even the physical condition of the witness. Add the difficulties we find in describing what we see or hear, and we have a compound of factors that make accurate representation improbable. Finally, remember that most of the witnesses sincerely believe that their description is the accurate one, and we are almost entering the realm of impossibility! Anyone who has attended a football match and reads the newspaper reports can verify this!

Life is a series of perceived events. Our senses receive information, we translate them into emotional and rational data, and we respond to them. All the factors we mentioned above, plus countless more, make up the sum of our response to these events. The objective factors of each event are immutable, but our subjective response is conditional and variable. Nowhere is this seen more patently than in the subject of depression. Lack of true perspective is a major contributory factor in reactive depression, and a major effect of all kinds of depression, hence the need for this chapter.

## Objective truth

Objective truth is the foundation of true perspective. Many people are depressed because they have lost the ability to focus on facts. One of the great ills of our age is the rejection of absolutes and the downgrading of objective truth. How we see something is considered to be more important than the object itself. We shall see in this chapter that how we perceive things is crucial to our well-being, but it is utter folly to believe that we can do so by devaluing the importance of objective reality. How we internalize and interpret objective truth determines how we feel and act towards it. The danger occurs, however, when we develop a mindset that simply sees what it wants to see. This appears to be the way in which many people approach life today.

When we think about it, even for a fleeting moment, we can see that this is the result of man's self-centredness. For example, we are told that religion is essentially experiential, and that we must not be dogmatic about doctrine. The creed of liberalism and religious pluralism is, 'Be at peace with your god, whatever you conceive him to be'. If we are uncomfortable with anything that is in the Bible, we are urged to re-interpret it or even reject it. 'Pick and mix' Christianity seems to be the order of the day. Many people go to church to 'experience' the presence of God, and yet come away no wiser as to the nature of his being. Truth is considered to be relative to the current needs or aspirations of the individual. This is not confined to religion; it has permeated every area of life.

Rejection of objective truth is disastrous. It takes away the foundation for everything that God has given us to build our lives (Matthew 7:24-27). The Bible teaches that our eternal destiny is not based on what we have discovered but on what God has revealed (2 Corinthians 4:3-4; 1 Peter 1:10-12); our morality should not be based on what we feel but on God's law (Judges 17:6; Matthew 5:17); our behaviour is not determined by the changing patterns of society but by the unchanging counsel of God (Psalm 1:1-2). The foundation of the gospel is the fact of Christ's redemptive work; his birth, life, death, and resurrection. The power of the gospel is the application of this fact to the life of the believer through the work of the Holy Spirit.

We cannot bring something into existence simply by believing that it is there. Eventually we are going to realize that we are left with nothing but an illusion. The people of the ancient world made their gods from wood, stone and precious metals; we are in danger of making the same gods from less tangible things.

We cannot change something simply by refusing to believe that it is not there. Neither can we hide from truth by refusing to see or hear it. Most children go through the phase of believing that if they cover their eyes no-one else can see them. Did any of us not put our fingers in our ears when being scolded by parents? We soon discovered the folly of this, but sadly, many of us still do this with objective truth that we find uncomfortable or unpalatable. There may be things in our lives that we do not want to think about or face. We can repress them, or cover them so well, it is as if they no longer exist; the trouble is, they do not go away.

Having said all this, we must not run away with the idea that perception is unimportant. The subjective element is as important as the objective, but it must always be subservient to it. This is the only way to gain a true perspective of things. Our perspective consists of facts *and* feelings. If we downgrade the importance of facts, we are left at the mercy of every emotional whim. If we do likewise with our feelings, and pride ourselves on our rationality, we overlook an important element of our being. Not to hold the two in balance is the cause of much unnecessary confusion and suffering.

## Subjective experience

The subjective experience of objective truth governs the way in which we live in this world. We feel and act on our current interpretation of situations. By removing or downgrading objective truth, we lay ourselves open to manipulation and exploitation. We see this clearly in the field of advertising. What we know about a product is considered to be less important than how we feel about it. The manufacturer, or his advertising agent, wants us to have an immediate emotional bond with his product. He knows that this is the most effective way of getting us to buy it! If we 'fall in love with it' we are less inclined to worry about whether we can afford it or not. Politicians, and others in public life pay great attention to their image. Gone are the days when a leader of a political party thought that its policies alone would make it electable. Even church leaders are urged to address the way in which their particular denomination or fellowship is presented to the world at large. We cannot deny that presentation is important, but it is equally important to keep it in proportion and not let it determine the content of that which is being presented.

Jung saw the dangers of this in the individual. We all have a persona, that is, the image we project to the people around us. This image is generally determined by social factors. When we take on a task, we also take on the role associated with that task. We expect people who exercise a certain function to 'look the part' and 'act the part'. We would be surprised if a plumber attended our house dressed in a three-piece suit, and used Latin terminology in describing the various parts of our water system! We would have little confidence in a lawyer who arrived in court dressed in overalls, calling everyone, 'Guv'! We all operate under different personas at different times; at work, at home, and even in the church. A crisis occurs when the persona is no longer congruous with the personality. In other words, when we are no longer true to ourselves when the role we are playing is the direct opposite of what we truly are. This was precisely the problem with the Pharisees. They were more concerned about what the world saw than by what God saw. This is why Jesus called them 'whitewashed sepulchres', and referred to them as, 'hypocrites', wearers of the actors mask. For most of us, the mask is thrust upon us by the expectations of others, and to some degree, we must wear it, but we must be ever mindful of its dangers. Some people become depressed because they genuinely feel that they have taken on so many roles, they no longer have room for themselves.

Perspective is gained from internalizing and interpreting the circumstances of our lives in the right way. You may be familiar with the saying, 'One man's problem is another man's opportunity', and there are many more along these lines. When we are depressed, we are, quite rightly, urged to think positively. The problem is, however, when we are depressed we can find nothing positive to think about! Why is this so? Simply because there is no power in positive thinking itself. The man who sees the opportunity instead of the problem is not necessarily just a positive thinker; he is someone who sees the circumstance from a different perspective. The man who sees the problem relates the circumstances to his lack of resources, inability, fear of failure, and general lack of confidence. The man who sees the opportunity does so from the perspective of one who believes that he may well succeed, and even if he fails, he will learn something! We cannot change our thinking without first changing our perspective. The author of a popular psychology book urges his readers to frequently repeat Paul's words, 'I can do all things through Christ who strengthens me' (Philippians 4:13). Positive thinking focuses upon the words, 'I can do all things', biblical perspective, upon 'through Christ who strengthens me'. I am not advocating the abandonment of positive thinking. We should all think positively. But, we cannot simply decide to think positively about what we perceive to be negative circumstances. Our perspective needs to change. This can only happen when we realize that our circumstances can be seen from a different viewpoint, and when we are prepared to include that view in the overall picture. All of us are limited in our perception. We can only see things from where we are, but this is not the complete picture. We can gain information from others, who see things from a different angle. This may be helpful, but we are still left with an unclear picture of events. How others perceive things may not necessarily be a true picture. We are all sinners, and we are subject to our own internal realization limitations. The Christian, however, has access to infallible, clear, and trustworthy data on all the circumstances of his life. He has God's perspective, revealed to him in the Scriptures. This is objective truth that becomes subjective reality when we 'read, mark, and inwardly digest' the word of God. This is no guarantee that we will never become depressed, for reasons I have outlined in earlier chapters, but it is a buffer against depression and is a healing balm in its midst.

## Perception

Perception determines our perspective. 'In essence, the study of perception always begins with recognition of the fact that what is perceived is not uniquely determined by physical stimulation but, rather, is an organized complex, dependent upon a host of other factors.'[1] What are these factors, and how can we relate them to depression? This is a study in itself, and outside the scope of this book, but there are three areas I want to highlight, that I believe will help us to understand the complexities of the process.

Firstly, *attention*. We are told that the human mind has the ability to receive and retain every piece of information fed into it. Our perception, however, is determined by the things we choose to focus upon. We have the ability to select these things from the countless stimuli we encounter every moment of our lives. If we sit on a train, absorbed in a book, we are only vaguely aware of what is happening around us. We have to take the deliberate action of pausing to check that we have not passed our destination. In the midst of a crowd of chattering people we are able to selectively listen to the person who is speaking to us. What we attend to, or focus upon contributes to the perception we have of the whole situation. When engrossed in what we are reading, the crowded environment of the train, delays between stations, and any other inconvenience has no effect upon our sense of well-being. If we close our book, look around, listen to the complaints of other passengers, and glance at our watch, we can easily become agitated and even angry. What we focus upon determines our perception of the journey.

The Bible has much to say about the things we focus upon. We are told to think of the true and good things, and meditate upon them (Philippians 4:8); to look to Jesus, 'the author and finisher of *our* faith' (Hebrews 12:2); and to look for his 'glorious appearing' (Titus 2:13).

Secondly, *interpretation*. What we make of what we pay attention to, also determines our perception. There are a number of factors involved in this process. If we view a familiar object from an unusual angle it does not alter our overall perception of the object itself. Our perception is greatly influenced by the angle at which we first saw the object. Our first impressions of people have a great effect on how we view them for the rest of our relationship. We may eventually change our minds about them but this does not come easily to us. Our first experience of a situation may determine how we approach similar situations in the future. Another factor is motivation. How we perceive something is influenced by how important it is to us at the time. A starving man sees a crust of bread as a banquet! We might throw it to the birds. When we feel vulnerable we tend to cling to the people who give us a sense of security. We must also take into account that what we perceive is influence by the state in which we perceive it. Our culture, background, learning experiences and emotional state all play their part in determining how we interpret what we see and hear. Objective reality takes on a size and proportion in relation to what we are comparing it with.

This leads us on to our final factor, *distortion*. Depression and distortion go hand in hand. In the earlier chapters of this book we recognized that physiological factors contribute to many cases of depression. We cannot dismiss the fact that God has given us a complex biochemical system. Any alteration in its balance has an effect on cognition and reaction. Perception is no exception. We must expect to perceive things in a different way when we are depressed. If we have a sound self-knowledge and acceptance, we are not daunted by this, even though it is unpleasant and disorientating. Distortion will clear and we will again perceive the events of our lives more clearly.

We must be careful, however, not to assume that distortion is always the result of biochemical change. We may become depressed *because* we have viewed events in a distorted way. The factors we have mentioned in the two previous headings may play an important part in this. We may have focused our attention on the wrong things; or we may be relating what we see to unhealthy and destructive habits of thinking. This may lead to a kind of neurotic paranoia, where everything we see and hear is perceived as threatening to our well-being.

# The eternal perspective

'Now faith is the substance of things hoped for, the evidence of things not seen'(Hebrews 11:1). The Christian has a perspective that sees beyond the temporal plane. Whatever the circumstances of life on earth, he has always been able to see beyond his physical and psychological limitations and fix his eyes on something greater. God has granted us eternal perspective. The Bible records times when this was even visible to the human eye (Acts 7:55-56; Revelation 1:10-12), but as a rule this perspective is gained through the eye of faith (John 20:29). The eleventh chapter of Hebrews speaks of many whose eyes were fixed on something greater than their present circumstance. We are told that, 'These all died in faith, not having received the promises, but having seen them afar off were assured of them, embraced *them* and confessed that they were strangers and pilgrims on the earth'(Hebrews 11:13). Their eyes were upon the eternal promises of God, and even though their circumstances often militated against them, and at times their faith wavered, they were *assured* of the promises, *embraced* them, and *confessed* them. The patriarch, Abraham, is the supreme example of this. The Lord Jesus Christ referred to him when he said that he, 'rejoiced to see My day, and saw *it* and was glad'(John 8:56). Abraham was literally a stranger and pilgrim on earth, yet in his heart and mind, 'he dwelt in the land of promise', and, 'waited for the city which had foundations, whose builder and maker is God'(Hebrews 11:9-10).

From my house, I can see central London stretched out before me. It is rarely an uplifting sight. Sometimes it is shrouded in mist, and looks drab and uninviting. On a warm summer day, a layer of pollution is often visible. The only time it has any great attraction is on a clear winter's night when the buildings are floodlit, and thousands of lights twinkle invitingly. I think of the millions of people I cannot see; many are lonely, some are homeless, most are teeming through its streets searching for entertainment and pleasure that will see them through to another day here on earth; very few have their eyes on the eternal city of God! I am momentarily depressed. Then I remind myself that God is at work. Unseen by my eyes, there is another picture that can only be seen by faith. In the midst of the city, God has people, who are praying, working and witnessing to the saving truth of the gospel, and that where sin abounds, grace abounds much more (Romans 5:20). I am able to rejoice that, in the city made by man's hand, someone has been found of God, and entered the city of eternal foundations. I can only see this through the eyes of faith, focused upon the promises of God in his word. My earth bound vision sees the city, and my imagination can only see the despair and hopelessness of the teeming masses.

We can easily become depressed when we lose sight of this truth. When we are depressed, this becomes increasingly difficult. How can we maintain the eternal perspective? We can only do so through focusing on the heavenly perspective we receive through the Bible. It is sad to say that many Christians only turn to the Bible in times of trouble and depression. We thank God that there is comfort to be found within its pages, but the right thing to do is to become familiar with God's truth *before* we need it in an emergency! When we are depressed, we have little energy or inclination to read anything. The Bible contains preventative medicine for the soul. It keeps us from being absorbed in and overwhelmed by the world of the senses. Those who are prone to depression, for whatever reason, can testify that the word, 'hid in the heart' has great efficacy, and enables them to put things into proportion. William Bridge has written, 'God has provided promises of comfort, succour and relief, suitable to all conditions. I dare boldly challenge all men to shew me any one condition for which God has not provided a promise of comfort, mercy and succour suitable unto it. Yea, and if you look upon the promises, and ponder them well, you shall find that they are so laid, worded and moulded, as that all discouraging objections may be fully answered, and taken away when they rise.'[1] If we are grounded in the Bible, we are able to deal with discouragements, 'when they rise'. Depression often gets a grip upon us when we fail to, or are unable, to do this.

## Contentment

Perspective leads to contentment. We are often discontent because we have failed to get things into perspective. This may be a factor in making us feel depressed. In many ways, depression and contentment are direct opposites. Herbert Carson puts this well when he says, 'If depression is existence in the shadows, then contentment is life in the sunshine'.[2]

The letter to the Philippians is the warmest and most personal document we have, among the apostle Paul's writings. It was written from prison in response to a gift and encouragement from the church at Philippi. In it, Paul says, 'I have learned in whatever state I am, to be content: I know how to be abase, and I know how to abound, Everywhere and in all things I have learned both to be full and to be hungry, both to abound and suffer need. I can do all things through Christ who strengthens me.' (Philippians 4:11-13). Here is the great charter of Christian contentment, and worthy of closer examination.

Paul has *learned* to be content. Many people see contentment in terms of temperament. Quiet, placid, easy going people who never say much, and always seem to be content. On the other hand there are those who are always striving for something greater, always pushing forward the boundaries of their lives. These people never seem to be content. This is a false idea about the nature of contentment. It has nothing to do with a person's temperament. The seemingly contented person may simply be lazy or apathetic. Striving after greater things is often a product of true contentment.

Why does Paul emphasize that he has learned to be content? It is because he is honest about his own weak and selfish nature. A seemingly contented person may be far from content. They may be the type of person who is able to hide their self-pity and their sense of the injustice of life. The stoics prided themselves on this. A person may seem to be content through fear. Locked into a situation or lifestyle that oppresses them, they submit to its pressures and exhibit a calm state that looks like contentment, but, in reality, is a front for a person who is desperately unhappy. Discontentment with what God has given us is essentially a sin. This is why contentment is an acquired rather than an inherent quality.

Some people view contentment in terms of *circumstances*. In doing so, they generally refer to it in the future tense, 'If I get that job, house, extra money. . . I will be content'. Of course, viewing contentment in this way is the very antithesis of contentment. We will never be content if we see it in future terms. Paul saw this clearly in his own life, 'Everywhere and in all things I have learned'. What had he learned? He had learned that contentment does not come from the circumstances, but from the one who is with him in the midst of the circumstances. This is why he is able to say, 'I can do all things through Christ who strengthens me'.

Paul has experienced poverty in its various forms. He knows how to be 'abased'. This literally means to be depressed or humiliated. Hendriksen translates it as 'straitened circumstance'. For the cause of Christ, the apostle had suffered many hardships and dangers; some of them humiliating and frightening (2 Corinthians 6:3-10). He knew what it was like to be hungry and in need. There is no virtue in poverty that will of itself produce contentment. There is a danger of romanticising poverty in the way that writers like Leo Tolstoy have done. Monastic vows seem to have a great air of virtue, but in reality this is no true poverty at all. The monk will never starve or be humiliated in his circumstances; in fact he will be revered by others for his self-sacrifice. Real poverty grinds away at the very foundation of all that makes up our well-being. To be content in the midst of it requires something greater than the poverty itself. Paul had learned this.

He also knew prosperity, to 'be full' and to 'abound'. He had been a prominent Pharisee, a position of great honour and respect. During his ministry as an apostle, there were times when he had been well cared for (Acts 16:15, 40; 28:2). Now, under Roman imprisonment, he was being cared for by the church at Philippi. Paul knows that prosperity can be more destructive to the soul than poverty. Prosperity can make us materialistic, and can divert our attention away from the eternal perspective. It can bring with it the fear of loss, a factor that plays a prominent role in depression. Whatever we possess, tangible and intangible, is subject to loss. If this is the case, can we ever know contentment? Paul shows us how we can do this by placing our loss into perspective. He does this by counting all the things he has as loss, before he loses them (Philippians 3:7-8)! As Archibald Hart says, 'This is why we need perspective on the large issues of existence. . . The perspective on life that God gives through faith in Christ can make the difference between whether we see loss as catastrophic or not'.[3]

We now turn to some positive advice on how we can get our circumstances into the right perspective.

# Focus

In the last chapter we learned the importance of eternal perspective. This enables us to put life-events in focus so that they will not distort our view of the whole picture of life as it is presented to us. In this chapter we will deal with four important factors that relate to depression.

## Learning to respond

Depression can be the result of inappropriate reaction to events. Hasty reaction is inappropriate where a considered response is called for. The wisdom books of the Old Testament emphasize this: 'Do not hasten in your spirit to be angry, For anger rests in the bosom of fools,'(Ecclesiastes 7:9). 'Do you see a man hasty in his words? *There is* more hope for the fool than for him'(Proverbs 29:20; see also 19:3; 21:5). In the New Testament, even the city clerk at Ephesus sees the wisdom in this (Acts 19:36).

We all have a tendency to jump to conclusions. As we have already discovered, we relate what we see and hear to internal factors and we interpret what we see through them. We have become so familiar with this, we often make the mistake of completing the picture before we have all the information. This is a verifiable psychological phenomenon. One of the most common representations of this is the drawing of a curved line that almost meets. Our immediate response is to see a circle. As we assume that the artist has intended it to be so, we automatically complete it for him. In fact, it is only a curved line. Most of the time, we do not realize we are even doing this. The following example will illustrate this.

For the last seventeen years I have been the pastor of a church in Brentford, Middlesex. I am aware that some people confuse this with Brentwood, Essex. I have lost count of the number of occasions in which this has happened. This is perfectly understandable. When it does happen, I go to great pains in making it perfectly clear that it is Brent*ford*, and not, Brent*wood*. Sometimes I even spell it out! However, it is not usually long before all is forgotten and I am introduced as Jim Winter from, Brent*wood*. For a long time I laboured under the conclusion that my diction was poor, or, even worse, that I was so insignificant nobody listened to a word I said! I was rescued from such psychological trauma by the organizers of a conference. I had dutifully filled in my application form in block capital letters, including the location of my church. Back came the booking confirmation and conference details—including a typewritten badge bearing the title, 'Jim Winter—Brent*wood*'!

As a general rule, this phenomenon has only minor, sometimes humorous, repercussions, but when it is carried forward into relationships the effect is far more serious. How many relationships have been damaged because explanations were not allowed to be completed, or actions have been misconstrued? Misunderstanding lies at the foundation of 'soap opera' scripts. Episodes abound with teenagers storming out on anxious parents half way through a conversation; or people, seeing others in perfectly innocent situation, jumping to the wrong conclusions. The stories that unfold often end in disaster. Without the misunderstandings there would have been little room for drama. Do we, however, want real life to be as dramatic?

Depression can so often be caused, or aggravated, by the same phenomenon. Relationships may be soured by misunderstandings and hasty words. Life events are only partially understood. Circumstances are interpreted before they unfold.

## Do not dwell on the past

When we are depressed, we often focus our attention on the past. David does this when he says, 'When I remember these *things*, I pour out my soul within me. For I used to go with the multitude; I went with them to the house of God, With the voice of joy and praise, With a multitude that kept a pilgrim feast'(Psalm 42:4). Looking back is part of true perspective. The Bible commands us to do this (Isaiah 46:8-9; 1 Corinthians 11:24-25), but we must not dwell on the past and make unhealthy and unwise comparisons between present circumstances and past events. The Bible tells us, 'Do not say, "Why were the former days better than these?" For you do not enquire wisely concerning this'(Ecclesiastes 7:10).

We are not to dwell on past blessings, other than to give thanks to God, or to remind ourselves of his providential care. To do so, is to blind ourselves to what God is doing in our lives at this present moment. It is far easier for us to look back and see what God has done than to detect his purpose in our present circumstances.

We must also be careful not to dwell on what would be considered as the negative factor in our past. We may have committed some great sin; we may have failed in a relationship; we may have been abused by another person; or we may feel that we have let God down. Past events may have been traumatic and left their residue within our personality, but it does us no good to dwell on them other than to deal with them in a proper and effective way. Past experiences still retain great power within us. If you want to test this hypothesis, just try remembering one of your most embarrassing moments! Have you started to blush yet?

## Be balanced

In some ways, the Christian life seems to be filled with excesses. Our right-eousness is to exceed the righteousness of the Pharisees (Matthew 5:20); we are to be 'exceedingly glad' when people persecute us (Matthew 5:12). God has given us, 'exceedingly great and precious promises'(2 Peter 1:4), and has promised to do 'exceedingly abundantly above all that we ask or think'(Ephesians 3:20). The Bible, however, warns us of the danger of the wrong kind of excess (Ecclesiastes 7:16-18).

The whole of God's creation is wonderfully balanced. 'While the earth remains, Seedtime and harvest, Cold and heat, Winter and summer, And day and night, Shall not cease (Genesis 8:22). The Christian life is a balance of weakness and strength (2 Corinthians 12:9-10); labour and rest (Luke 13:24; Matthew 11:28-30); gain and loss (Philippians 3:7); and shadow and sunshine (Psalm 30:5; Revelation 7:14-17). The mountain-top experience of the disciples was balanced by the need that awaited them in the valley (Matthew 17; Mark 9).

Balance is essential to a healthy life. We must eat a balanced diet and pay attention to the amount of rest and exercise we get. We must learn to be balanced in the way that we perceive the circumstances of our lives. Things do go wrong, but they do not *always* go wrong. There is a danger of making sweeping generalizations about things, and invariably they are in the negative and not in the positive frame.

Chapter 19

## Do not be over-sensitive

'Do not take to heart everything people say, Lest you hear your servant cursing you'(Ecclesiastes 7:21). Our perception is impaired when we become oversensitive to what people say or do. Depression often highlights this. A thoughtless word or action can often cause a depressed person to burst into tears. Can we do anything about this? We can take preventative measures that will dissipate its power over us. We all get hurt by criticism or by what people say about us. We must not, however, take these things to heart. We have already discovered that it is a human trait to speak critically about others, especially when they are not there. This is why the writer of Ecclesiastes goes on to say, 'For many times, also, your heart has known That even you have cursed others'(Ecclesiastes 7:22). Many of us would be ashamed if others knew of the things we said about them when they were not there. If we had to explain our action, we would say that we either spoke in a fit of anger; or we did not really mean what we said; or we were simply having a bad day and did not have a good word to say about anyone. This may well have been true, but the damage will have been done. We must beware of the power of the tongue (James 3). The thing we must bear in mind is that when people speak ill of us, their explanation would probably be the same! If we are over-sensitive we will dwell on every word. If we have received the information through a third party, we will dwell on every misquote!

Some people place themselves in situations that almost cry out for an over-sensitive reaction. The husband who rummages through his wife's handbag is not in the right frame of mind to interpret the significance of what he finds. I am amazed at the way some people plead with others to tell them what they *really* think, then become upset when they do!

We have examined the importance of, and the way in which we can gain a true perspective of life. The following chapters will help us further in this matter.

# God's pattern for life

Every living being needs rest and recreation to maintain the balance for a healthy life. For the human being, this must include physical, mental and spiritual needs. How we approach this in practice is determined by our occupation, age, health, family commitments and other responsibilities. A person with a sedentary occupation will have to pay attention to his physical well-being by taking some form of appropriate exercise. A person who is called upon to expend vast amounts of physical energy will ensure that he takes adequate periods of rest. Someone burdened with great responsibilities will learn to 'switch off' and occupy his mind with less stressful activity. Whatever the individual requirements, each situation is unique, hence the need to know ourselves and our circumstances. Overriding all of this is our need to draw close, and stay close, to the God who created and redeemed us.

Failure to understand and implement this balance is a serious health issue. Our bodies and minds can only take a finite amount of pressure; when overloaded they will respond by shutting down. Any number of stress related diseases may ensue. Prominent among these will be depression.

How do we ensure that our lives have this balance? Our requirements and experiences may vary, but the principles, however, are constant, and this is what we will be examining in the following three chapters.

### God's provision

'Remember the Sabbath day, to keep it holy. Six days you shall labour and do all your work, but the seventh is the Sabbath of the Lord your God. *In it* you shall do no work: you, not your son, nor your daughter, nor your male servant, nor your female servant, nor your cattle, nor your stranger who *is* within your gates. For *in* six days the Lord made the heavens and the earth, the sea, and all that *is* in them, and rested the seventh day. Therefore, the Lord blessed the Sabbath day and hallowed it' (Exodus 20:8-11). The God who created the earth has set in motion a principle that provides for its total well-being. For mankind, the pinnacle of his creation, he has given ten commandments that will ensure that the priorities for a healthy, happy, godly life are kept. The fourth commandment deals with how we prioritize and spend our time.

For many, time is a tyrant. It dominates every day. The busy person seems to be in its clutches from the time the alarm clock wakes him in the morning until he returns, weary, to his bed at night, regretting that he still did not have enough time to complete the intended tasks of the day. We intend to spend more time with our families; to give more time to others; and most importantly, spend more time alone with God. Each failure of our intention seems to be mocked by the clock! For the sick, lonely or depressed person, time weighs heavily upon him. For many, it is the case of getting through another night, or another day. The eternal God is the Lord of time. Our time is in his hands (Psalm 31:15). Time is the most precious commodity we have in this life, surely it is the first thing we ought to entrust to the wisdom of our heavenly Father. The founder of Harvard University, Thomas Shephard, said, 'Time is one of the most precious blessings which worthless man in this world enjoys; a jewel of inestimable worth; a golden stream, dissolving, and, as it were, continually running down by us, out of one eternity into another, yet seldom taken notice of until it is quite passed away from us. Man (saith Solomon) knows not his time (Ecclesiastes 9:12). It is, therefore, most just and meet that He who hath the disposing of all other things less precious and momentous should also be the supreme Lord and Disposer of all our times.'[1]

This commandment will be the main focus of this chapter. I will deal sparingly with the biblical and theological reasons why the Lord's Day must be observed, in order to concentrate on the factors that are especially relevant to our study. For a good treatment of the subject in general, I recommend John Thackway's, *The Lord's Day—principles and practice*.[2]

## The Sabbath principle

The Sabbath principle deals with man's relationship to his environment. The physical world is naturally recreative. Enshrined in the work of creation is a principle established for all time (Genesis 2:2-3). The only blot on the landscape is sinful mankind. God has given man dominion over his creation (Genesis 1:28). With the appearance of sin, this dominion of benevolent care has been threatened by the spectre of exploitation. Human intelligence and resourcefulness, allied to inherent greed, if left unchecked, leaves creation at man's mercy. The results, as we can see around us, are devastating. To check this, God has commanded man to implement a Sabbath principle in the use of his natural environment. The word *Sabbath* means to cease or rest. This was not just for man's good but also applied to his beasts of burden (Exodus 20:10; 23:12). The sabbatical year was implemented so that the land may rest (Exodus 23:10-11; Leviticus 25:1-8).

The Sabbath principle also deals with man's relationship with his fellow man. There was a release from servitude. No one should be made to work on the Sabbath (Exodus 20:10). Restraints upon work, however, do not apply to acts of mercy (Matthew 12:10-13; John 9:14).

The Sabbath principle deals, ultimately, with man's relationship with God. He has set aside one day in seven to be his day (Exodus 35:2). As Thackway says, 'He has fenced it off from the other six days and declared it to be divine property'.[3] It is the declaration that God is in control and that his wisdom is greater than ours. He has revealed that it was created for our well being, 'The Sabbath was made for man, and not man for the Sabbath'(Mark 2:27). To keep the Sabbath means that we are entrusting our well-being to his wisdom.

## The Lord's Day

There are many books that deal with the Christian practice of a first day Sabbath. This book will add little to the argument. There are strong biblical reasons we are to set aside the first day of the week to the Lord. The Christian's focus is upon Christ, as God's revelation to man (Hebrews 1:1-3). He declared himself to be 'Lord of the Sabbath' (Mark 2:28). He did not come to abolish the law, but to fulfill it (Matthew 5:17). The fulfilment of the Sabbath law is to be found in him. As Thomas Watson has said, 'The grand reason for changing the Jewish Sabbath to the Lord's Day is that it puts us in mind of the "Mystery of our redemption in Christ," The reason why God instituted the old Sabbath was to be a memorial of the creation; but he has now brought the first day of the week in its room in memory of a more glorious work than creation, which is redemption.'[4] Christ rose from the dead on the first day of the week (John 20:19). On the next first day, he revealed himself to Thomas, as the disciples gathered together (John

20:26). The church set aside the first day for worship and giving (Acts 20:7; 1 Corinthians 16:2). The important point to make, for the purpose of this book, is that the Sabbath principle and Sabbath laws apply to the Lord's Day. Christ did not come to abolish, but to fulfil. As the Bible tells us, 'There remains therefore a rest for the people of God. For he who has entered His rest has himself also ceased from his works as God *did* from His'(Hebrews 4:9-10).

## God's blessing

The Lord's Day is a day that is blessed by God. For the child of God it is the most blessed and happiest day of the week. God has promised great joy to those who keep it (Isaiah 58:13-14), yet many Christians appear to have forgotten this, or, having been seduced by an ungodly attitude towards time, have chosen to ignore it. Many of us are under intense stress, but we are mistaken if we think that we can alleviate our stress by stretching the working week into seven days instead of six. The effect is the very opposite. For most, this is not a conscious decision—the Lord's Day becomes eroded and not eradicated. Provision is made in God's word for the necessary work that must take place on the Sabbath, but it is easy for unnecessary activities to subtly encroach upon his day. At first, we may simply try to 'fit in' the tasks that we have failed to complete during the week. We soon discover that they increase. We may occasionally miss a service of worship because of this. We have every intention of going to church, but things are taking longer than we envisaged. There are many more social activities and events that now occur on the Lord's Day. Many of them involve our children. Do we attend them? We may decide that from time to time it will be all right to do so. These times become more frequent.

The computations of this scenario are endless. The effect, however is the same. By stretching our week in this way we have contributed nothing to our well-being. In fact, the very opposite has taken place. We are more tired, more stressed, and worst of all, the blessings we once knew are no longer there. I have yet to meet one person who has done this and ended up the better or happier as a result

We may justify our decisions by reminding ourselves that we do not want to be legalistic about how we spend the Lord's Day. In doing so we miss the point of it all. Our motive for keeping this day is love for God and gratitude for his grace. The Puritans were greatly misunderstood about their attitude towards the Lord's Day. They have often been branded as 'legalistic' or even 'killjoys'. If we read their works, we soon develop an understanding that they emphasized the Lord's Day for reasons other than legalism. Richard Baxter sums up their position when he writes, 'What fitter day to ascend to heaven, than that on which He arose from earth, and fully triumphed over death and hell. Use your Sabbaths as steps to glory, till you have passed them all, and are there arrived'.[5]

God has promised a blessing to those who keep his day. To withdraw from the obligation to keep the day means that we are withdrawing from the blessing. To withdraw from the blessing is to retreat into a state of being that leaves us open to the physical, psychological and spiritual causes of depression.

Whatever argument put forward to support the erosion of the Lord's Day falls at the first hurdle. It denies the wisdom of God and elevates the foolishness of man. We will now examine some of the positive blessings that God bestows upon those who keep his day.

# Rest and recreation

The Lord's Day is a day of rest. Many people misunderstand the true meaning of rest. Rest cannot be achieved solely through physical inactivity. Our bodies can be perfectly still, but our hearts and minds can be engaged in frenzied activity. An evening slumped in front of the television set can be an exhausting experience. The quality of rest is more important than its quantity. Jesus summed up true rest in the words, 'Come to Me, all you who labour and are heavy laden, and I will give you rest. Take My yoke upon you and learn from Me, for I am gentle and lowly in heart, and you will find rest for your souls'(Matthew 11:28-29). The Lord's Day provides us with positive rest. It is a time when we can consciously discard the yoke of secular activity and take on the yoke of Christ. A day when we can actively seek him without the distractions of our legitimate worldly responsibilities. Even when we are busy in the Lord's work, his day is a day of rest, for we must remember that the fourth commandment sets us free from 'labour'. A day spent in worshipping, seeking, and serving God is the antithesis of labour. Even the Department of Health recognizes that, 'having a spiritual dimension to one's life helps those with mental health problems and depression'.[1] The Lord's Day is more than a spiritual dimension, it is a governing factor. In this context, keeping the Lord's Day has a 'knock on' effect for every day of the week. By consciously setting aside this day in obedience to God, we are made to realize that we *can* take control of our use of time, and that we can choose to rest during our weekly labour. Not only this, but we learn that rest is essential so that the labour may be effective.

It is important that we also make adequate allowance for rest in a busy week. Some of us may need to learn a relaxation technique that we can practise during a busy day. We must be careful, however, to choose one that does not embrace New Age philosophies or paraphernalia. People under undue stress or facing depression generally have to make changes in their life-style. The first question they should ask is, 'How do I spend the Lord's Day?'

## Recreation

'I believe that Sunday should be spent in recreation. You are dreadfully shocked, and well you may be. But what do I mean by "recreation"? It means creating us new. Oh, that everybody who talks about spending Sunday in recreation would come to be recreated, regenerated, renewed, refreshed, revived, and made to rejoice in God.'[2] These words were written over a hundred years ago, yet they are strikingly relevant for our day. The kind of recreation referred to by the writer is not the same as that which now dominates the nation's use of the Lord's Day. Christians who wish to participate in, or watch sports are increasingly finding that they can no longer do so and honour God. All kinds of recreational activities now occupy our Sundays instead of our Saturdays. Many children can no longer take part in certain team sports unless their parents allow them to do so on the Lord's Day. Many 'role model' Christians in sport and entertainment pay little regard to the Sabbath. Charities now focus many of their fund raising activities on the Lord's Day. Increasingly, Christians are surrendering to the pressures of the world, and participating in these things. Again, for reasons we have outlined in the previous section, this erodes the individual's observance of the Sabbath. Apart from the fact of breaking the fourth commandment, it is detrimental to our well-being.

The Lord's Day is a day of recreation. It is an institution of creation and an agent of re-creation. Taking part in healthy physical activity, visiting an art gallery, or raising money for a good cause may do us some good, but not at the expense of the recreational blessings that God has prepared for those who keep his day. To take time to engage in worship, to spend time in unhurried prayer, to feed upon God's word, to enjoy the fellowship of fellow believers, to give thanks for our temporal and eternal blessings, and to play our part in the furtherance of his kingdom is true recreation. The Lord's Day is a day when the wounds of the previous week are healed, and strength is gained for the week ahead.

## Worship

The Lord's Day is primarily a day of worship. Worship is directed towards God alone; it is God-ordained, God-directed, and God-centered. In true worship, we seek to please God and not ourselves. Our needs, wants, likes or dislikes have no part in it; neither should our current mood govern our attitude or actions. By its very nature, worship is a wonderful form of therapy. The paradox is, that once we begin to treat it as such it loses its therapeutic power. Worship that is geared to the needs of the worshipper becomes no more than a religious group therapy session! We do not worship in order to feel better about ourselves. Although this may have a temporary beneficial effect, it has no lasting substance, as it simply drives us deeper into self-centredness. The beneficial effects of worship come only when we do not seek them. This principle is enshrined in the words of Jesus, 'For whoever desires to save his life will lose it, but whoever loses his life for My sake will save it'(Luke 9:24).

The Westminster Shorter Catechism tells us that, 'Man's chief end is to glorify God and enjoy him for ever' How can we best glorify God? Thomas Watson list four things that are essential in this: Appreciation, adoration, affection, and subjection.[3]

We appreciate God when we focus our attention on who he is. In doing so, our hearts and minds are lifted to a higher plain. When we consider his attributes: his independence (John 5:26), unchangeableness (Malachi 3:6), eternity (Psalm 90:2), ever-presence (Psalm 139:7-10), knowledge (John 21:6), wisdom (Psalm 104:24), goodness (Psalm 86:5), love (John 3:16), grace (Nehemiah 9:17), mercy (Romans 9:18), longsuffering (Numbers 14:18), holiness (Exodus 15:11), righteousness (Psalm 89:14), faithfulness (Numbers 23:19), sovereignty (Ephesians 1:11), will (Deuteronomy 29:29), and power (Job 42:2), we are 'lost in wonder love and praise'. We cannot appreciate God until we take time to consider who he is. Appreciation comes through the realization of an object's value. If God becomes the 'object' of our attention he will be valued above all things. As the Psalmist says, 'For You, Lord, *are* most high above all the earth; You are exalted far above all gods'(Psalm 97:9). This turns our attention away from the 'gods' of our lives, the things that dominate our thoughts and drain our energies, and whose loss will lead us into depression.

Appreciation leads naturally on to adoration. This is true worship. We are commanded to worship God in holiness (Psalm 29:2), in spirit and in truth (John 4:24), and in a way that is acceptable to him (Hebrews 12:28). The Westminster Confession of Faith tells us that, 'The light of nature showeth that there is a God, who hath lordship and sovereignty over all; is good, and doeth good unto all; and is therefore to be feared, loved, praised, called upon, trusted in, and served with all the heart, and with all the soul, and with all the might'. When we worship God our hearts and minds are to be solely set upon him. It is difficult to switch off the negative thoughts that so often occupy our minds. The most effective thing to do is to replace them with more powerful positive thoughts. There are a number of psychological techniques that help us do this. The key factor is, that the new, positive thought must be more attractive, loom larger in our imagination, and be accompanied by a great sense of joyous anticipation. Do I need to spell it out? What could be more attractive, greater, joyous, and glorious than setting our hearts and minds upon God in adoration and praise?

We glorify God in the love we have towards him. The apostle Peters says of Jesus Christ, 'Whom having not seen you love. Though now you do not see *Him*, yet believing, you rejoice with joy inexpressible and full of glory'(1 Peter 1:8). We do not need to introduce the 'feel-good factor' into worship. True worship is the expression of love for God, and abounds in 'joy inexpressible'.

In his great work, *A treatise concerning religious affections*, Jonathan Edwards deals comprehensively with the nature of religious emotion. He takes great pains to point out the dangers of equating true religion with religious experience. This does not mean, however, that we are to suspend emotional activities whenever we enter into an act of worship. Edwards observes that, 'True religion consists, in great measure, in vigorous and lively actings of the *inclination* and *will* of the soul, or the fervent exercises of the *heart*'.4 Worship expresses and increases our love for God. Are we not moved when we join together in heartfelt praise? Or when we hear the gospel preached? Worship is the most profound and pure of emotional experiences. In it our emotions become servants instead of tyrants.

To worship God is to serve him. We are subjects of the heavenly king. This gives all our lives meaning and purpose. We can easily become depressed when we feel that our lives are meaningless. We may question our purpose here on earth and find none. Watson's astronomy may be suspect, but his spirituality is not, when he writes, 'A good Christian is like the sun, which not only sends forth heat, but goes its circuit round the world. Thus, he who glorifies God, has not only his affections heated with love to God, but goes his circuit too; *he moves vigorously in the sphere of obedience* [italics mine]'.5 Worship cannot be contained in the act alone. It sends us forth with a divine purpose. When we contemplate the nature of our God, cast ourselves in adoration before him, and warm our hearts at the fire of his presence, we are motivated by a renewed desire to move our lives into conformity with his will.

At the close of this section, I must repeat and re-emphasize that worship is not intended to be a form of therapy. We must never approach it with the idea of what we will get out of it. What I have done in this section, is to point out the wonderful therapeutic effect that true worship brings. We will never gain this effect by seeking it. My advice would be to forget what you have read in this section, and get on with the duty and joy of simply worshipping the Lord!

## Fellowship

'And let us consider one another in order to stir up love and good works, not forsaking the assembling of ourselves together, as *is*, the manner of some, but exhorting *one another*, and so much more as you see the Day approaching'(Hebrews 10:24-25). The early Christians were noted for their desire to meet together, to worship and enjoy the fellowship of each other's company (Mark 1:21; Acts 2:44-47; 13:14). Christ has promised his own presence with those who do this (Matthew 18:20; 1 Corinthians 1:9).

We all live and work with people who do not share in nor understand our relationship with God. Most of us have non-Christian friends whom we love, and who love us. We have many things in common with them, but we cannot share the same perspective. The Christian is in the world, but not of the world (John 17:11-18). Although we have the promised presence of Christ, we can still feel isolated as we go about our daily duties in a world that rejects the Saviour. God has given us a means by which we can be strengthened and supported—the fellowship of the saints.

In an earlier chapter I noted some of the problems that occur when people come together in close fellowship. We are all sinners and, as a result, there will always be misunderstandings and problems with our relationships, but, I must emphasize that the blessings far outweigh any problems that may occur. I would go as far as to say that many of the problems themselves are blessings in disguise.

The nature of fellowship is one of receiving and giving. We are recipients of the grace of God, and the power of that grace is expressed within the life of the church; having received from God, we also need to learn to receive from each other. For most of us, receiving is more difficult than giving. By receiving, we are releasing others into the joy of giving, and also releasing ourselves from a spirit of independency that is unhealthy and unholy. It is easy to criticize others for not giving, when we ourselves, have erected barriers of unreceptiveness. This, eventually, can lead us down the road of self-pity.

Giving is an essential part of fellowship. Jesus said, 'Freely you have received, freely give'(Matthew 10:8). The church is to come together in a spirit of giving (Acts 4:34; 1 Corinthians 16:2). By giving we acknowledge the Lordship of Christ over all that we are and have. I remember reading a popular psychology book where the writer urged his readers to practise the art of tithing both time and money. He suggested that by giving a tenth of our time and money to the needy, we release our minds from the burden of being controlled by either. In doing so, we will reap the rewards of prosperity. The Christian tithes from different motives, but the effect is the same, even though the rewards may be different.

Giving involves more than putting our money in the offering on the Lord's Day. In the very act of coming together, we give each other our attention. In doing so, our minds can no longer be focused solely upon our own needs and difficulties. A Rabbi, perturbed by the way in which many members of his congregation were complaining about the heaviness of the burden each had to bear, decided on a course of action. He announced that there would be a special service where they would all bring their burdens to the synagogue and lay them before the Lord. After they had done this, they proceeded to discuss the nature of each person's burden, and offer prayers for God's strength. At the conclusion of the service, each person was invited to pick up the lightest burden and carry it home. Without exception, everyone went home carrying the burden they had brought!

In Christian fellowship, we are able to bear each other's burden and encourage each other along the way. The very act of doing this enables us to put our own problems and difficulties into perspective, and ultimately causes us to realize how blessed we really are.

None of the things we have mentioned in this chapter are 'cure alls' for depression. They are, however, principles that, when put into practice, enable us to build healthy and holy lives that will enable us to be strong in the Lord. If, for whatever reason, we become depressed, we will have some God-given resources with which to deal with it.

# Help!

The second half of this book has largely been taken up with ways in which we can prevent depression and minimalize its effect. We have compared it with a tangled chain, and have gently stroked it along the way. By now the knots should have been loosened, enabling us to complete the untangling process. To do this it may be necessary to seek help. These final chapters deal with the help that we may need.

There are some general points to be made before we look at specific ways in which we can find help. We hope and pray that, during the course of this book, we have been able to highlight areas that can be addressed and dealt with before we reach the stage where we seek further help. Understanding the nature of depression can often be the means by which we untangle ourselves from its grip!

In previous chapters, I have said little about the person and work of the Holy Spirit. As an evangelical Christian I am confident that he who indwells every believer will be the agent of our restoration, whatever the cause of our depression, and whatever means are required for our recovery. Deeply aware of the inadequacy and fallibility of the words I have written throughout this book, I firmly believe that the Spirit of grace and truth is at work in every individual Christian, and those who are truly coming to faith in Christ. It is essential for us to trust in his wisdom and to constantly pray for understanding as well as for relief.

The kind of help required will depend on the stage we have reached. As depression deepens and intensifies, the range of treatment becomes more specific. John White helpfully sums it up, when he writes, 'The treatment a depression calls for will vary according to its nature and severity. In its initial stages at least, depression is not one thing but several. We have enough evidence now to realize that the more serious a depression becomes, the more it will resemble any other depression as it converges with the "final common pathway". Like tributaries that arise hundreds of miles apart to converge into one great river, depressions differing widely at their sources become progressively more similar in their pathology. The more serious the depression, the better is its response to physical measures (antidepressant medication and ECT).'[1]

We have already examined some of the tributaries. We will now look at the main river itself; depression. as a *state* rather than a *mood*.

## Recognising our need for help

When depression is a mood, brought upon by our present circumstances, we are generally able to rationalize it and deal with it ourselves. We know that this feeling of inadequacy, unhappiness, or worry is only transient and will eventually pass. However troubled we may feel, we know that the storm will abate and we will again be on calmer waters. Our circumstances will often determine the length and depth of our depressed condition. For many it will only be a matter of days before the depression lifts; for those who are bereaved it will be a long, slow process. We have to recognize, however, that there may be times when our mood does not lift as we expected and the depression we are experiencing has become a state. In other words, we are saying, 'This is how I *am*', rather than, 'this is how I *feel*.' It is at this point that we must recognize and acknowledge our need for help. Family and friends often see this before we do.

There are a number of factors that complicate this process. These arise from the tangled nature of depression, and our tendency and ability to mask it. In its early stages, we may feel the need to hide it from others. It is understandable that most of us are reluctant to admit to our condition. There may be many reasons for this. We may not want to worry our loved-ones. We may be in a position of authority, where others rely on us for their well-being. To admit to depression may give them cause to lose confidence in us or weaken our effectiveness. We may not want to admit to weakness or helplessness. We may be fearful of our future prospects, if we admit that we have some kind of 'mental' illness. The Christian leader or worker may be anxious about the effect upon the life and witness of the church, especially if our theology does not allow for depression to be considered anything other than sin or unbelief. We may even feel that we have let God down! On the other hand, we may simply not understand the nature of depression, and ascribe our condition to some other cause.

We must be mindful that, in the early stages of depression, a specific behaviour can be a symptom or a mask. It may be the direct result of the depression itself, or it may be used to direct attention from the depression. For example, if a generally reliable person starts to miss appointments and make excuses for failing in their responsibilities, it may be that they are trying to hide their condition from others, or they may have lost energy and interest as a result of their depressed state. Whether a behaviour is a symptom or a mask, it is important for friends and colleagues to be aware that it could be an indication that the person is exhibiting signs of depression.

When we mask depression, we are not necessarily trying to be deceitful. Masking is often a misguided protective reaction to an increasingly threatening experience. Many people mask depression as a kind of therapy for their condition, believing that denial may cause it to go away!

In listing some of the common ways in which people mask depression, we must emphasise that the individual behaviours listed are not just specific to depression—they may have other causes. It is when such things are in combination and are relative to the classic symptoms listed in chapter one, that we can move nearer to a correct diagnosis.

When children become *unusually* apathetic, *excessively* disobedient or untruthful, they may be masking depression. This may be manifested in truancy or school phobias that do not have an obvious reason. Adolescents may exhibit similar symptoms or masks, but also turn to alcohol or drugs. Adults are a little more sophisticated in their masking techniques. Many complain of 'physical' disorders, taking time off work with bouts of 'flu' or an undiagnosed viral infection. Some visit their doctors complaining of various aches and pains that seem to defy diagnosis. A depressed person may resort to increasing their intake of painkillers or other prescribed medicines. Excessive use of alcohol is often a masking device; as is compulsive gambling and extramarital sex.

Whether our behaviour is a mask or a symptom, and whatever form that behaviour may take, recognition of the state of depression has to take place so that appropriate help may be given. To admit that there is a problem, and to recognize our inability to handle it on our own is a powerful therapeutic action. Although the depressed person may not feel an immediate benefit, it will give great relief to those who love and care for him. The next step is to decide what kind of help we need.

## Medical help

A person who is suffering from bipolar or manic depression is in need of psychiatric treatment. Someone with this condition is subject to violent mood swings, from being highly elated and full of energy to being plunged into the depths of despair. This condition is relatively rare and outside the scope of this book.

The vast majority of those who enter a state of depression have unipolar depression, which means that they are subject to an ongoing depressed condition from which there is no apparent relief. If we reach a point where the 'talking cure' is not sufficient to lift our condition, or if the one who is helping us feels that further help is necessary, it is advisable to seek medical help. Medical help and advice are always appropriate if a depressed person is exhibiting suicidal tendencies or speaking of a desire to end their own life!

A visit to the doctor can be beneficial for a number of reasons. Firstly, because our general state of health may be a major contributory factor. Our condition may be affected by a recent illness, or the result of chemical or hormonal imbalance caused by a current illness for which we are being treated.

Secondly, symptoms of depression may also be recognized side-effects of medication we may be taking for an unrelated condition. Thirdly, because, whatever its initial cause, disruption of biochemical mechanisms in the brain is now considered to be a major factor in depression.

A skilled medical practitioner will be able to detect the need for further treatment or change prescribed medication. He will also be able to prescribe anti-depressant medication that will help the chemical imbalance that has taken place. There are a number of Christians who are reluctant to take medication for depression. This is understandable, in the light of the fear of anything that tampers with the natural cognitive and emotional balance of the brain, and also the fear of addiction to anti-depressants. If, however, we accept that depression has its own physiological peculiarities, we should not reject, out of hand, any means by which these can be balanced. Most of us are perfectly happy to take medication for more obvious physical conditions. Many Christians have been helped through the critical stages of depression by the careful use of anti-depressant medication. Taking an anti-depressant is not a resignation that our faith has failed or that we have placed ourselves entirely in the hands of secular humanism. If we are so depressed that we are unable to cope with life, and we are making those around us miserable, then medication may well help provide the right mental and emotional environment in which we can deal with the underlying causes of our condition. We must, however, be cautious in our use of medication. Anti-depressant drugs are powerful and may have strong side-effects. It is wise to talk these matters over with our doctor before we embark upon a course of treatment. We must also recognize that they only provide part of the answer to our problem. There is a danger that, if we are taking anti-depressants, as the depressed mood lifts, we may no longer see the need to address its source!

## The 'talking cure'

The phrase, 'talking cure' is reputed to have been coined by Bertha Pappenheim, one of the first patients to claim successful treatment through psychoanalysis. She later went on to become a well-known humanitarian relief worker. Pappenheim used the term to describe the therapeutic effect of working through her problems verbally. Its use has spread to describe other kinds of therapy that centre upon the need for a patient to talk through his condition. We must not underestimate the power of talking and listening. Recent medical studies have suggested that the very act of talking things through with the right person in the right conditions has a remarkable effect upon brain chemistry. The effect produced is similar to, and in some cases more effective than anti-depressant medication. It also has the advantage of fewer side-effects!

It would be easy to generalize about whom we should or should not talk to, but, in my experience, this is often determined by the circumstances in which we find ourselves. There are obvious priorities and ideals, but the severity of our condition and the availability of the right kind of help sometimes takes things out of our own hands. We must remember, however, that we are still in the hands of God and that he will not abandon us in our need. Although it was not told for this express purpose, the story of the 'Good Samaritan' shows us that sometimes it is the 'wrong' person who is the greatest help.

Having said this, it is right and proper that we seek help from someone competent to minister to us in our condition. This person should be a mature fellow believer; someone whose faith and practice are rooted and grounded in the Scriptures; who will be both sympathetic and constructive; someone who is godly, humble and 'down to earth'; who will keep a confidence and in whom we can have confidence. The New Testament teaches us that this kind of ministry is expected to be part of normal church life. We are all called to 'weep with those who weep'(Romans 12:15); to 'bear one another's burdens' (Galatians 6:2); and to 'comfort one another'(1 Thessalonians 4:18). The elders of the church are instructed to encourage, care for, and minister to the flock (Titus 1:9; 1 Peter 5:2); especially to those who are sick (James 5:14).

It may be helpful, and sometimes necessary, to talk to someone who is trained and experienced in dealing with depression. There are two cautionary notes that must be sounded here. Firstly, our confidant must be sympathetic with our Christian beliefs. We have dealt with the dangers of 'selfism' in a previous chapter. Some counsellors may try to instil a set of values that are contradictory to Biblical teaching. Some may even view our faith as being a contributory factor to our depression! Whatever 'expert' help we receive must be held up to the light of biblical truth. Secondly, we must be cautious in our use of Christian counsellors. While there are many sound, Bible based, practitioners, there are also those who consider themselves 'spiritually gifted', and who, with little understanding of the nature of depression and with scant regard for biblical principles, submit their 'victims' to a bombardment of quasi religious or psychological theories.

When we have found the right person to talk to, what do we talk about? Firstly, we will need to be able to express how we feel. This may not be as easy as it sounds. We may have become so numbed by our state that we feel that we have no feelings to express; or it could be that we have always been reluctant to talk about our feelings for fear of being judged or rejected. This can, in itself, be a contributory factor in our depression. Sometimes we are afraid of saying how we feel for fear of being challenged to produce a reason. We may be reluctant or unable to respond. Once we have gained confidence in the person we are talking to, we will be able to begin to unburden our fears, anxieties, anger, doubts, sins, and all the other destructive elements of our condition. However painful this may be, knowing that the person we are talking to is listening patiently and sympathetically will be of great help to us. Unburdening in this way can be an exhausting but wonderfully therapeutic experience.

Secondly, we need to talk about our circumstances. These will have played a dominant role in causing our condition. Our concerns about our spiritual state, health, family circumstances, work, financial situation, and a host of other things may come to the surface. We may need to talk about how we feel about ourselves. As we talk through each issue we will feel more able to address it and discuss how we are going to face and deal with it. Knowing that we have someone on our side, who will offer help or point us in the right direction, will encourage us to believe that all is not lost. This will help us put things into perspective.

Thirdly, we will need to talk about our spiritual condition. When in the depths of depression, God may have seemed far away. As we emerge, we become aware that he has not forsaken us. He was there all the time, and his hand was upon us, even during the darkest hours. Our faith may have taken a buffeting, but this was permitted in order to strengthen rather than destroy us. We must now learn to build on this experience and go on with the Lord even stronger than when we first became depressed. We must give ourselves again to prayer, worship, and Christian service. We may have to deal with besetting sins or address our relationships with other Christians. Whatever needs to be done, we need someone who will gently lead us back into discipleship, praying with us and for us, returning us to the Word of God, and encouraging us to take our rightful place in the fellowship of his people.

Fourthly, we may need to address wrong thinking or behaviour. This may be an area that has contributed to our depression. We may still be prone to react inappropriately to events. In this book we have dealt with attitudes toward the self, and perspective. We may need to examine our attitudes toward others and the ways in which we inter-relate with them. For some, assertiveness may be an important area.

Fifthly, we may need to examine our lifestyle and learn practical ways in which we can deal with stress.

We can do many of these things on our own, but for some we may need professional guidance.

# Family, friends and fellowship

D epression can have a draining effect upon those who are closest to us. In this sense, it is a contagious disease. If we are living with, or having close daily contact with a depressed person, we have a two-fold problem. Not only are we trying desperately to help the one we love, we are also having to deal with the effect upon our own well-being. It is important to recognize this and not allow the situation to get on top of us. How can we best do this?

We must try, as much as possible, to have a strategy by which we deal with the situation. There is a great danger that our moods will fluctuate violently from sympathy to anger. We are naturally sympathetic towards the person who is suffering, but we will soon find that this has little effect on their condition. A depressed person is usually full of self-pity, and sympathy alone often encourages them to continue in this state. Herbert Carson uses the following analogy, 'The sympathetic friend feels rather like a gardener using a watering can on a blazing hot day where the water evaporates before it even penetrates the soil. A little reflection may lead to the realization that wise gardeners do not water plants in the blazing sunshine! So there is a wiser way of showing sympathy that helps rather than hinders'.[1] If we show sympathy alone, it will not be long before we become impatient and angry. This, too, will have a negative effect on a depressed person, by making them feel more helpless and guilty than they already do! It is crucial that their moods do not control ours. By taking calm control of the family situation, we create the right kind of environment in which recovery will take place. This is not easy, and requires great patience and self-control. It is important that carers have respite from the pressure, are able to talk through their problems and difficulties with others, and have a safe means by which they can express their frustration or anger away from the depressed person.

When a person is depressed it affects every member of the family. A marriage will be placed under stress, when a spouse will not be able to function as a helpmeet or sexual partner. This may produce great frus-tration in the relationship, where the confidences and worries of the nondepressed partner have to be temporarily shelved, and there is little or no interest in the physical expression of mutual love. Children are greatly affected when either mother or father is depressed. This is exacerbated when they do not understand the change in behaviour of the depressed person. They may feel unloved, unwanted and rejected. When a child or teenager is depressed, this causes great worry to parents and often resentment on the part of siblings. The family routine is affected by disrupted sleep patterns, mealtimes, and the usual weekly activities. Routine chores are not completed, bills are not paid, and the whole well-being of the family seems to be under threat.

Sympathetic action needs to be taken. Firstly, members of the family need to discuss the situation. The depressed person must not be excluded from this, although there may be occasions when it will be necessary to re-appraise the situation without them being present. It is important, however, that they do not feel that everyone is talking about them behind their backs! At the outset, the problem needs to be recognized and accepted by every family member. Children, depending on their age and ability to understand should have the situation explained to them as clearly as possible. We have already looked at the ways in which a person may mask their depression. It is important that there are no 'family masks'. We must not make the mistake of denying the reality of the situation for fear of causing more disruption. This never works. Depression can only be dealt with on a personal or family basis when it is brought into the open. By trying to hide it in the home we are giving it a stigma or a power that will only be destructive. Every family member knows that something is wrong; it is best that the wrong is identified, so that it can be addressed by everyone.

Secondly, it is essential that no blame is attached to anyone at this point. It is easy for the depressed person to be blamed for their behaviour. It must be pointed out that such behaviour is the result of their condition. We would never expect a wife or mother to function normally as she recovered from a serious illness; neither would we expect a father, son or daughter, to mow the lawn if they had a broken leg! Neither should blame be attached to any particular family member. It is easy to look for scapegoats. Even if the behaviour of one of the family members has been a factor in the depression, this is not the time for accusation. We are not conducting a trial, but having a discussion on how best we can pull together and help the situation. Individual family members should not take the blame upon themselves. This will only multiply the problem and make recovery of normal family life more difficult. If there is any blame to be apportioned, it should be dealt with at a later stage.

Thirdly, a sensible, practical strategy should be implemented. When a family member is depressed, particularly a mother or father, responsibilities and tasks will have to be shared by others. These must be sensibly allocated and accepted. They must also include the depressed person. This, of course, will depend upon the nature and extent of the depression. It is important that we do not treat the depressed person as an invalid. We must however try to encourage them to do simple tasks, express gratitude when they do, and try not to show anger when they try and fail.

Fourthly, we should take an interest in, and be supportive in their treatment. If they are taking medication, we must be aware of the side-effects, but encourage them to continue their medication. If they are receiving counselling, we must never pry. A spouse may be suspicious and even afraid of what their partner is telling the counsellor. There is a danger that some family members may see such counselling as a betrayal of family confidence. This is not the case and we must not be resentful.

Fifthly, it is important that we support each other. This will be a time of great stress for every family member. We do well to monitor our own progress as well as that of the depressed person.

Sixthly, we need to pray with and for the depressed person and for each family member. Although our prayers will focus much upon the needs that arise from each situation, they should be full of praise and thanksgiving for every little victory.

Depression is exceedingly stressful on the family, but it is also a time when bonds can be strengthened and individuals can mature. By facing the problem together we can forge a unity that will have a lasting effect on every family member. Future family celebrations will have a deeper joy.

## The fellowship of believers

The church is our extended family. For many lonely and depressed people it is their only family. In a previous chapter we addressed some of the negative aspects of fellowship as they affect someone with depression. We said then, and we repeat now, that these are far outweighed by the positive, therapeutic benefits of the fellowship of the saints. What can we do to help a fellow believer who is depressed? We will address the question in three stages: the general effect of church life; specific attitudes and actions; and the help we receive from the wider church.

A healthy church has much within its life and activity that has a positive beneficial effect. We are instructed in the Scriptures to, 'Consider one another in order to stir up love and good works, not forsaking the assembling of ourselves together, as *is* the manner of some, but exhorting *one another*'(Hebrews 10:24-25). The services of worship focus our attention on God. They remind us of his greatness; lift our eyes from the temporal to the eternal; point us to the Lord Jesus Christ, our Saviour and Lord. The Lord's Table brings home the reality of our redemption; binds us together in a common bond of commitment; and bids us look for his coming. The preaching of the Word challenges and encourages us. The meetings for prayer enable us to participate in the wonderful interaction between God and man through our great high priest. A depressed Christian may not feel a desire to worship or attend any church activities, but must be encouraged to do so. We may even feel that we are being hypocritical in attending, but by continuing to do so, we are in the best environment for healing.

The most telling time for the depressed person is the moments before or after worship. How should we approach him? We should do so with loving sympathy, enquiring how he is feeling, not being perturbed if we get little response, or if he bursts into tears. Our ministry to him should simply be an expression of our love and support. This is not the time for a mini counselling session or prayer meeting! Our approach should be brief and sensitive (unless the person requests further conversation). Often, where appropriate and proper, a simple touch is all the person needs. Most of us will feel that we can do nothing or have anything helpful to say, but we must not underestimate the power of our caring presence.

It is also helpful to offer practical support to the depressed person and their family. This is often appreciated more than 'spiritual' forms of ministry.

It is important, however, that we do not try to take over. We may feel that a trip to the countryside or a shopping expedition may take the depressed person out of themselves. We must be careful that we are being helpful and not imposing another burden on someone who is already feeling over-burdened. Offers of help should simply be offers of help and no more.

Like the family, we should be supportive in the treatment the person is receiving. It can be distressing for a depressed person to know that there is conflict within the fellowship over treatment received. If we do not agree with the approach being taken, we should be quiet unless asked for our opinion. Even then we should be sensitive and diplomatic. We should also refrain from speculative or critical comments made to other members of the fellowship. It is amazing how quickly things get back to others.

We should pray together for the depressed person, their family, and those who are seeking to help him. Receiving the united encouragement of the fellowship will play a large part in recovery.

We can be greatly helped through the writings of Christians who have experienced depression. To read of how someone like C. H. Spurgeon coped with and triumphed over depression can be a great tonic. It is helpful for us to know that many saints whom God has used for his glory have encountered and suffered from forms of depression. There is a danger of feeling that we have become useless in the Lord's work, and forfeited the right to ever serve him again. Yet when men of the stature of Samuel Rutherford can write, 'I am at a low ebb as to any sensible communion with Christ; yea, as low as any soul can be, and do scarce know where I am'[2], we know that all is not lost.

We can also take encouragement from the great hymns. Many of these have been written in the midst of adversity. One of the great hymn-writers, William Cowper, suffered severe bouts of depression during his life and ministry yet he could write,

Ye fearful saints, fresh courage take;
The clouds ye so much dread
Are big with mercy, and shall break
In blessings on your head.

George Matheson, author of O Love that wilt not let me go, and, Make me a captive Lord, lost his sight during his late teens. Charlotte Elliott, an invalid for the last fifty years of her life, wrote, *Just as I am—without one plea*, on a day when she was feeling particularly unwell and depressed. Henry Francis Lyte wrote, *Abide with me*, whilst terminally ill. The great hymns of Isaac Watts, Charles Wesley and John Newton, echo across the centuries with words of comfort and hope for the depressed believer. They also offer a mild rebuke to us when we are simply feeling sorry for ourselves. It is no great wonder that the Bible exhorts us to admonish one another, 'in psalms and hymns and spiritual songs' (Colossians 3:16).

When I am feeling depressed I derive great comfort from re-reading books that have been a blessing to me in brighter times. It is useful to store up material that we know will minister to us during our dark days. Martyn Lloyd-Jones placed on record his indebtedness to the writings of Richard Sibbes during a time when he was overworked and badly overtired.[3] The church, past and present, has a wealth of comfort and help for those who are depressed.

# God's Word

Throughout this book we have taken the position that the Bible is the ultimate authority for faith and practice. We bring it to a close by looking at ways in which it helps us when we are depressed. We have seen that whatever the origin or cause of depression, it has not severed the Christian's relationship with God. For some, it may even have been a means of bringing us into that relationship.

In the preceding pages we have looked at many passages of Scripture. In this final chapter we will focus upon three particular areas where we can find great comfort and help during our darkest hours.

### The ministry of Jesus

The Bible teaches that God, who revealed himself in the person of Jesus, fully understands the nature of human suffering. During his ministry here in the flesh, the Son of God was, 'A man of sorrows and acquainted with grief' (Isaiah 53:3). He wept over the death of a friend (John 11:35), and over a city that rejected him (Luke 19:41). He knew what it was to be 'despised and rejected by men' (Isaiah 53:3).

As we read through the Gospels we are struck by the empathy he had with the suffering, and the tender way he ministered to them. This is emphasised in the way in which he is described as being 'moved with compassion', when facing a needy crowd (Matthew 9:36; 14:14; 15:32); when responding to the pleas of a leper (Mark 1:41; and when meeting a grieving widow (Luke 7:13). He showed the same compassion when confronted by the violent self-destructive behaviour of a demon possessed man (Mark 5:19). It is wonderful to know that he who is the same, yesterday, today and forever (Hebrews 13:8), has the same compassion on us when we feel like lepers, suffer the torment of loss, or feel self-destructive. His is not the helpless sympathy of one who stands by and watches us suffer, but the compassion of one who has entered human suffering, ascended victoriously, and who stands at the right hand of God to intercede on our behalf (Hebrews 4:15). When I am feeling depressed, I take great comfort in Christ's fulfilment of Isaiah's words, 'A bruised reed

He will not break, And smoking flax He will not quench, Till he sends forth justice to victory'(Matthew 12:20; Isaiah 42:3). Richard Sibbes describes him as, 'A physician good at all diseases, especially at the binding up of a broken heart; he died that he might heal our souls with a plaster of his own blood'.[1] When we are depressed, it is helpful to read through the Gospels and simply watch the Lord Jesus Christ at work among the wounded souls of his time, knowing that he continues his work in us through the Holy Spirit's application of his finished work on the cross.

When we are depressed, it is also helpful to remind ourselves of some of the comforting and practical things our Lord said. He invites us to come to him (Matthew 11:28), and promises that he will not turn us away (John 6:37). He draws our attention to the providential care of God in the natural world and compares it with his Father's care for us (Matthew 10:28-31). From similar observations he instructs us to make some important changes in our thinking (Matthew 6:19-34). We are to *prioritize*. We may be depressed because the pressures of life are getting on top of us. Often, this affects our walk with the Lord. This is the real cause of our depression. We have got our priorities wrong. Jesus tells us not to, 'lay up for yourselves treasures on earth', but to 'lay up for yourselves treasures in heaven'. The antidote to worry is to get our priorities in the right order by seeking first God's kingdom. God will provide the means by which the things of earth will be dealt with. For someone who is depressed, this has a two-fold effect. It gives us *one* thing to focus on in the midst of a jumble of anxieties. It also deals with our sense of helplessness. When we are depressed we are caught up in the spiral of being unable, even unwilling, to face the problems that confront us. We can become more depressed at the thought of our situation deteriorating because of our neglect. To know that by one action we can be sure that someone is in control can have a profound effect upon our well-being. God will take care of us and our circumstances, often through the help of caring friends, and sometimes in ways that will astound us! When we are depressed, we need to 'go back to basics'. Here is a basic truth that needs to be stated, re-stated, and then repeated, until we take it deep into our being. We can all testify to circumstances in our lives that have really brought home to us the truth of a particular Bible passage.

Jesus also teaches that we must learn to *compartmentalize*: 'Therefore do not worry about tomorrow, for tomorrow will worry about its own things. Sufficient for the day *is* its own trouble'(Matthew 6:34). Here is another basic truth that is crucial to us in depression. Worries and regrets about the past, and fears for the future, spill over into the present, burying us beneath their load. Disturbed sleep patterns, that often accompany depression, tend to blur the edges of each particular day so that time becomes one continuum instead of daily compartments. It is important to re-establish as much of a daily routine as possible. What is crucial in this, is that we allow ourselves time, in the confines of each day, to address our worries and fears concerning that day. When we are depressed we have the tendency to swing from worrying about everything to trying to dismiss all worry from our minds. In doing so we are never able to address the practical ways in which we can deal with the things that are causing our depression. Daily compartmentalization has another beneficial effect. When we are depressed, we are often locked into a syndrome of joylessness. We feel we cannot, and sometimes we are determined not to, enjoy anything. This is not surprising, as we feel that we are in an endless spiral of anxiety. By regaining the *day* we have a short sweep of time in which we can properly assess events and experiences. Looking back over a day, we may be able to point to one or more things that have brought us pleasure. Maybe it was a simple thing like the first cup of tea of the morning; or some task that we were able to perform with a little satisfaction; a short conversation with a friend or family member; a favourite hymn that we sang in church; or any thing that, even momentarily, brought a smile to our faces. However small or fleeting the experience, it shows us that light is breaking through into our darkness! We must deliberately look for these things. The self-destructive, self-pitying, nature of depression will try to blind us to them.

### The Psalms

In times of darkness, the Psalms have brought strength and comfort to God's people throughout the ages. Martin Luther took courage from the words of Psalm 46, 'God *is* our refuge and strength, A very present help in trouble'. Augustine had an inscription of Psalm 32 above his bed so that his eyes would alight upon it when waking. In death, John Calvin was said to have uttered the opening words of Psalm 13, 'How long, O Lord?', and friends sang Psalm 102 to the dying David Brainerd.

Many depressed people have found great comfort from the book of Psalms. It has been called, 'the songbook of the depressed'. In it we find the expression of and the remedy for our wounded feelings. In this book we have used Psalms 42 and 43 to describe the nature of depression, and to show how we should address it. David, having described his feelings, goes on to show how he will ultimately triumph over them. Both Psalms end with the same words, 'Why are you cast down, O my soul? And why are you disquieted within me? Hope in God; For I shall yet praise Him, The help of my countenance and my God'.

Psalm 102 has the same descriptive and therapeutic elements. The Psalmist describes his depressed condition honestly and graphically, but is ever looking to God for his deliverance, 'But You, O Lord, shall endure forever, And the remembrance of Your name to all generations. . . But You *are* the same, And Your years will have no end'(Psalm 102:12 and 27).

William Cowper, who suffered agonising bouts of depression received great help from the Psalms. As a boy, bullied at school, he was strengthened by the words, 'The Lord *is* on my side; I will not fear. What can man do to me?'(Psalm 118:6). Later in life, when recovering in an asylum after a suicide attempt, he was able to say, 'The Lord *is* my strength and song, And He has become my salvation'(Psalm 118:14).

Sinclair Ferguson's book, *Deserted by God*, is very helpful to someone seeking comfort and help from the Psalms.[2]

## Prayer

When we are depressed, we ought to pray. We often find it difficult; and sometimes even impossible. It is comforting to know that others are praying for us, and helpful when someone prays with us. We should not be daunted by our inability to frame our thoughts and feeling into the right words. We do not need to inform God about our condition; he knows more than we can ever know. By simply trying to pray we are opening ourselves to the unrestricted channel between earth and heaven in Jesus Christ. We have the comfort of knowing that the Holy Spirit, 'helps in our weaknesses' and 'makes intercession for us with groanings which cannot be uttered'(Romans 8:26). Our most feeble attempts at prayer will not fall on deaf ears.

In our attempts at prayer we can take heart from the experience of David and Job, 'My tears have been my food day and night' (Psalm 42:3), and, 'My eyes pour out *tears* to God' (Job 16:20), knowing that the Lord responds to the tears of his people. He did so for David and Job, and he will for us! The Lord responded to Hezekiah's tears with the words, 'I have heard your prayer, I have seen your tears' (2 Kings 20:5; Isaiah 38:5). Through the prophet Isaiah, God gave a great promise to a repentant people who would rest in him, 'You shall weep no more, He will be gracious to you at the sound of your cry; When He hears it, He will answer you' (Isaiah 30:19).

In our depressed condition, we may fear that our Lord is no longer with us. We can take great heart from Mary Magdalene's experience in the garden. Grief stricken by the death of her Lord, she is devastated by the discovery that his body is missing. She hears the words, 'Woman, why are you weeping? Whom are you seeking?' When the risen Lord speaks her name, she is filled with joy inexpressible (John 20:1-17).

Christ will not abandon us in our depression. He will never leave nor forsake his people. Whatever the cause, and whatever means the Lord uses and blesses to bring us through its darkness we *will* emerge into the light. 'Weeping may endure for a night, But joy comes in the morning' (Psalm 30:5). We must cling to this great truth, even in our darkest hour, for truth it surely is.

## Notes

### Chapter 1 notes

1  **Milligan, S. and Clare**, **A.**, *Depression and how to survive it*, Ebury Press, 1993, p.36
2  **Reber, A. S.**, *Dictionary of Psychology,* Penguin, 1985
3  **White, J.**, *The Masks of Melancholy*, Inter Varsity Press,1982, p. 76
4  **Radcliffe, M.**, *Nursing Times, November 4-10*, 1998
5  **Bridge, W.**, *A Lifting up for the Downcast*, Banner of Truth Trust, 1995, p. 29
6  **Spurgeon, C. H.**, *The Treasury of David,* Passmore and Alabaster, 1876, p. 299

### Chapter 2 Notes

1  **Wilkinson, G.**, *Depression*, Family Doctor Guides, Equation in association with the British Medical Association, 1989, p. 18
2  **Gillett, R.**, *Overcoming Depression*, Dorling Kindersley, 1987, p. 19
3  **Gillett, R.**, *Overcoming Depression*, Dorling Kindersley, 1987, p. 24

### Chapter 3 notes

1  **Lloyd-Jones, D. M.**, *Old Testament Evangelistic Sermons*, Banner of Truth Trust, 1995, p. 3
2  **Spurgeon, C. H.**, *Autobiography Volume 2,* Banner of Truth Trust, 1983, p. 195
3  **Milligan, S., and Clare,** A, *Depression and How to Survive it*, Ebury Press, 1993, p. 69
4  **Jung, C. G.**, *Modern Man in Search of a Soul*, Ark, 1989, p. 99

### Chapter 4 notes

1  **Hart, A. D.**, *Coping with Depression in the Ministry and Other Helping Professions,* Word Books,1984, p. 40

### Chapter 5 notes

1  **Lee, R.S.**, *Freud and Chrstianity*, Penguin Books, 1969, p.141

# Notes

### Chapter 6 notes

1    **Milne, B.,** *Know the Truth,* Inter Varsity Press, 1996, p. 109
2    **Berkhof, L.,** *Systematic Theology,* Banner of Truth Trust, 1976, p. 670
3    **Watson, T.,** *A Body of Divinity,* Banner of Truth Trust, 1974, p. 152

### Chapter 8 notes

1    **Owen, J.,** *Works Volume 3,* Banner of Truth, 1966, p. 428

### Chapter 9 notes

1    **Davies, G.,** *Stress: The challenge to Christian caring,* Kingsway Publications, 1988, p. 134
2    **Reber, A. S.** , *Dictionary of Psychology,* Penguin, 1985, p. 313
3    **McKenzie, J. G.,** *Guilt: Its Meaning and Significance,* George Allen and Unwin, 1962, p. 34

### Chapter 10 notes

1    **Brooks, T.,** *Precious Remedies Against Satan's Devices,* Banner of Truth Trust, 1997, p. 16
2    **Lloyd-Jones, D. M.,** *Spiritual Depression,* Marshall Pickering, 1998, p.19
3    **Brooks, T.,** *Precious Remedies Against Satan's Devices,* Banner of Truth Trust, 1997, p. 168-170
4    **Ryle, J. C.,** *Holiness,* Evangelical Press, 1979, p. 105
5    **Thomas, I. D. E,.** *A Puritan Golden* Treasury, Banner of Truth Trust, 1975, p. 22
6    **Anderson, C.,** *Spurgeon: His life and legacy,* Unpublished Lecture.

### Chapter 11 notes

1    **Benfold, G.,** *Why Lord?,* Day One, 1998, p. 8-9
2    **Carson, D. A.,** *How Long, O Lord?,* Inter-Varsity Press, 1993, p. 9
3    **Luther, M.,** *A Commentary on St Paul's Epistle to the Galatians,* James Clarke, 1978, p. 553
4    **Spurgeon, C. H.,** *The Treasury of the Bible Vol. 3,* Baker Book House, 1981, p. 96

### Chapter 12 notes

1   **Beeke, J.,** *Sword & Trowel*, The Metropolitan Tabernacle, 1999 No.1, p. 16
2   **Vitz, P.,** *Psychology as Religion*, Lion, 1979, p. 9
3   **Johnston, M.,** *Child of a King*, Christian Focus, 1997, p. 151

**Chapter 13 notes**

1   **Thomas, I. D. E.,** *A Puritan Golden Treasury*, Banner of Truth Trust, 1975, p. 17
2   **Lockley, J.,** *A Practical Workbook for the Depressed Christian*, Word Publishing, 1991, p. 197
3   **Spurgeon, C. H.,** *New Park Street Pulpit 1858,* Banner of Truth, 1964, p. 400-461
4   **Lockyer, H.,** *All the Promises of the Bible*, Pickering and Inglis, 1962, p. 326
5   **Lloyd Jones, D. M.,** *Studies in the Sermon on the Mount*, Inter-Varsity Press, 1978, p. 79
6   **Swinnock, G.,** *Works Volume 2*, Banner of Truth, 1992, p. 131

**Chapter 14 notes**

1   **Sibbes, R.,** *Works, Volume 1,* Banner of Truth Trust, 1973, p. 144
2   **Lloyd-Jones, D. M.,** *Spiritual Depression*, Marshall Pickering, 1998, p. 20
3   **Baxter, R.,** *The Selected Practical Works of Richard Baxter,* Blackie and Son, 1840, p. 3
4   **Anderson, R. S.,** *New Dictionary of Christian Ethics and Pastoral Theology,*
    Inter-Varsity    Press,    1995, p. 772
5   **Lloyd-Jones, D. M.,** *Preaching and Preachers,* Hodder and Stoughton, 1976, p. 167
6   **Baxter, R.,** *The Selected Practical Works of Richard Baxter,* Blackie and Son, 1840, p. 13

**Chapter 15 notes**

1   **Prime, D.,** *Sermon on John 21,* Preached at Charlotte Capel, Edinburgh,
    4th October 1987

**Chapter 16 notes**

1   **Adams, J.,** *The Biblical View of Self-Esteem, Self-Love, Self-Image*, Harvest House,
    1986, p.        79
2   **Griffin, E.,** *The Life and Sermons of Edward Griffin*, Banner of Truth Trust, 1987, p. 176
3   **Chantry, W.,** *The Shadow of the Cross*, Banner of Truth Trust, 1981, p. 7

# Notes

4   **Griffin, E.,** *The Life and Sermons of Edward Griffin*, Banner of Truth Trust, 1987, p. 179
5   **Lloyd-Jones, D. M.,** *Spiritual Depression*, Marshall Pickering, 1998, p. 20

**Chapter 17 notes**

1   **Reber, A. S.,** *Dictionary of Psychology*, Penguin Books, 1985, p. 527

**Chapter 18 notes**

1   **Bridge, W.,** *A Lifting Up for the Downcast*, Banner of Truth Trust, 1995, p. 51
2   **Carson, H.,** *Depression in the Christian Family*, Evangelical Press, 1994, p. 96
3   **Hart, A. D.,** *Coping with Depression in the Ministry and Other Helping Professions*, Word Books, 1984, p. 85

**Chapter 20 notes**

1   **Shephard, T.,** *Theses Sabbaticae*, Soli Deo Gloria, 1992, p. 25
2   **Thackway, J.,** *The Lord's Day—principles and practice*, Day One, 1996
3   **Thackway, J.,** *The Lord's Day—principles and practice*, Day One, 1996, p. 6
4   **Watson, T.,** *The Ten Commandments*, Banner of Truth Trust, 1995, p. 96
5   **Thomas I. D. E.,** *A Puritan Golden Treasury,* Banner of Truth Trust, 1977, p. 171

**Chapter 21 notes**

1   *The Times,* London, 24/7/99
2   **Carter, T.,** *Spurgeon at his best*, Baker Book House, 1988, p. 119
3   **Watson, T.,** *A Body of Divinity*, Banner of Truth Trust, 1974, p. 7
4   **Edwards, J.,** *Works Volume 1*, Banner of Truth Trust, 1979, p. 237
5   **Watson, T.,** *A Body of Divinity*, Banner of Truth Trust, 1974, p. 9

**Chapter 22 notes**

1   **White, J.,** *The Masks of Melancholy*, Inter-Varsity Press, 1982, p. 188
**Chapter 23 notes**